# YEATS
*at work*

# YEATS
## *at work*

ABRIDGED

## CURTIS B. BRADFORD

THE ECCO PRESS

NEW YORK

Copyright © 1965 by Southern Illinois University Press

This edition first published in 1978 by The Ecco Press, Ltd.
1 West 30th Street, New York, N.Y. 10001
Distributed in Canada by Penguin Books Canada Limited

(The original edition contained material on Yeats's
plays and prose writings.)

The Ecco Press logo by Ahmed Yacoubi
Designed by Andor Braun

Published by arrangement with Southern Illinois University Press
Printed in the United States of America

**Library of Congress Cataloging in Publication Data**

Bradford, Curtis Baker, 1911–1969.
    Yeats at work.

    Includes bibliographical references.
    1. Yeats, William Butler, 1865–1939—Criticism,
Textual.   2. Yeats, William Butler, 1865–1939—
Technique.   I. Title.
[PR5907.B72  1978]      821'.8      78–5630
ISBN 0–912–94660–1

IN MEMORY OF

Professor H. O. White

1885–1963

# PREFACE

WRITING WAS ALWAYS DIFFICULT for Yeats. When he began in the 1880's he was prolix. The manuscripts of such unpublished apprentice works as have survived show little revision, but these plays, stories, and verses are loose, thin-spun, tedious. Yeats began to publish in 1886, but only a few of the works published before 1895 seem to have satisfied him; these early published works were either abandoned or carefully rewritten before they were included in the various collected editions. By 1895 Yeats had developed more effective habits of work; he now began to put both prose and verse through many drafts, to stick with poem, play, story, or essay until much hammering had worked it into shape.

Yeats's apprenticeship as a poet ended, as Thomas Parkinson has shown in *W. B. Yeats: Self-Critic*, when he revised his early verse for *Poems*, 1895. The legends and lyrics printed with *The Countess Kathleen* (1892) are clearly the work of a man who is forming a style whereas the poems collected in *The Wind Among the Reeds* (1899) display one of Yeats's styles fully formed. Yeats himself must have felt that this was so, for he continued to revise his early poems through many successive editions; the text of *The Wind Among the Reeds* remained, to the contrary, remarkably stable. During these same years Yeats completed his apprenticeship as a prose writer. For me, the stories included in *The Celtic Twilight* (1893) show an apprentice hand whereas parts of *The Secret Rose* (1897) do not. "Rosa Alchemica" is a finished work and, again, Yeats must have felt that this was so, for during the course of many reprintings he made very few changes in its text.

The road to a master's certificate as a playwright was both longer and harder: Yeats's whole practice of playwriting shows him intent on developing antirealistic dramatic modes. He achieved the first of these in his early heroic plays based on traditional Irish themes, but it took him more than twenty years to do it (he began planning *The Countess Cathleen* in 1889 and he finished the rewriting of *The Hour-Glass* in 1913; by that time all his early plays except *The King's Threshold* had reached pretty much the form in which we know them). He invented a second mode, the heroic farce, while at work on *The Green Helmet*, and in the version of that play published in 1910 we reach the moment of relative textual stability which Yeats had reached in his poetry with *The Wind Among the Reeds*. He went on to invent a third mode, the most successful of all, when he completed and produced in 1916 *At the Hawk's Well*, his first play for dancers.

Even though Yeats achieved mastery of the technical means of his art rather early in his career, he at no time found the act of writing easy. It was for him always an "unnatural labour." Yeats worked as hard at his writing in the 1920's and 30's as he had in the 1890's. Up to about 1920 his method of composing was physically tedious. He wrote always in longhand, very slowly, revising as he went along. Before his marriage he wrote usually in bound manuscript books, often cheap copy books intended for school exercises. He never at any time in his life produced a prose manuscript that could be transcribed by a secretary so Yeats's customary practice was to dictate from his manuscripts. Only two of all the prose manuscripts I have examined have been transcribed ("The Speckled Bird," and parts of "The Tragic Generation" and "The Stirring of the Bones"), and both transcriptions are extremely inaccurate. Verse manuscripts were, I believe, usually transcribed because of the difficulty of indicating line ends during dictation. When the manuscript on which he was working became nearly illegible because of overwriting and cueing in from the margins and the opposite page, Yeats would either copy it out, dictate it to a secretary, or have it transcribed. He always introduced further changes while rewriting or dictating. If Yeats had dictated or had a work transcribed, he would go to work on the manuscript or typescript his secretary had produced, carrying on in his own hand the process of revision. There was much work to be done on such a draft. Since Yeats was thrown off completely if interrupted while dictating, his secretaries had to write what they thought they heard; when transcribing they sometimes misread his writing. There are still many places where Yeats's printed texts inaccurately represent his original intention because his various secretaries misheard what he said or misread his hand, and Yeats happened to miss the mistake while correcting.

After his marriage Yeats worked out with Mrs. Yeats's help a method of composition that was less demanding physically. Now he usually wrote in looseleaf notebooks, except when he was away from his Dublin study, at Coole, for instance, or in Italy. When away from home he continued his earlier practice of writing in bound manuscript books. Looseleaf notebooks had one great advantage. Throughout his life Yeats continually rearranged the order of his material while composing, especially when he was writing prose. When he wrote in a bound manuscript book, he had to indicate by notes the order he wanted, or tear out or cut out the pages (Yeats did this even with books, including his own books) he wished to put earlier or later. Loose leaves were more easily rearranged. Often a looseleaf manuscript page will have at the top a series of page numbers indicating the various places it has occupied in a work.

When Yeats had achieved something of the order and style he wanted, he would, as he had earlier, dictate the work to a secretary or have it transcribed — he greatly preferred to work with Mrs. Yeats. He had by now developed a truly remarkable ability to improve both his prose and verse while working on these typed versions. Sometimes successive typescripts were needed, each dictated as the preceding script grew illegible: this happened with *A Vision* and *On the Boiler* (1939). But often in the 1920's and 30's Yeats finished his writing on the first typescript.

We have seen that Yeats nearly always wrote in a book either bound or looseleaf; apparently he liked the two-page spread each opening provided. He usually started on the right-hand page; when this became too overwritten, he would move over to the left-hand page and continue his revision there, cueing the passage into its proper place on the right-hand page by drawing arrows. Another aspect of Yeats's practice is worth noting, since it is often a source of confusion. When Yeats wrote in a bound manuscript book, he rarely used the sheets in order. He would move from place to place in the book, or both forward and back from the page on which he had begun to write. This means that the order of drafts, particularly drafts of poems, often cannot be determined by the order in which they occur in the book. When, finally, Yeats felt reasonably satisfied with a work, he would usually initial it, or even sign it in full, "W. B. Yeats," and often add the date. When a manuscript written in a looseleaf notebook had once been dictated or transcribed, Yeats would remove the sheets and put them into a file envelope. He would sometimes note the principal contents on the flap of the envelope, and the date of filing.

Yeats's manuscripts and typescripts are extremely interesting to any student of the writing process, for it is nearly always possible to reconstruct from them at least the external aspects of how a poem, play, or essay was put together. One can also watch lines of poems and single sentences of prose emerge from the inchoate as Yeats achieves with immense labor the expression he wants. For Yeats the construction process usually meant adding on; his works accumulated slowly, as a coral reef accumulates. The "First Draft," for instance, of the *Autobiographies* is a manuscript of about 42,000 words. The material in "First Draft" parallels "The Trembling of the Veil" (1922) and parts of "Dramatis Personae" (1938); these run to nearly 100,000 words. In poem or play as well as prose work, such a result is typical. The things added were usually detail, incident. Though some early drafts are too encumbered with detail, most of them show, as Yeats often complained, that his writing at the outset of a work tended to be abstract. In a lyric the rich fabric of metaphor and symbol as well as Yeats's characteristic staging of a poem builds up slowly through many drafts. This was notably true of "Sailing to Byzantium." In his play *The Resurrection*, what was little more than a dialogue on the nature of God slowly becomes a play with dramatic tension and climax. In "The Trembling of the Veil" Yeats slowly envelops certain personal reminiscences with the rich fabric of his System.

Yeats's characteristic styles were also achieved with difficulty; this is equally true of the hushed, autumnal tone of *The Wind Among the Reeds*, the splendid baroque diction of the great poems of the 1920's, and of the crackling, slashing sentences of the late prose works. In plays the adjustment of word and phrase to the actor's speaking voice was given minute attention, and plays were seldom printed until after production. After a certain point in the composition of nearly all his works, Yeats's revisions are largely concerned with improving the style.

There were exceptions to these usual procedures: During the many years he spent working on *The Player Queen*, Yeats accumulated a great deal of material he had to discard, including many pages of verse and much hard-worked-for incident. Yeats wrote many conclusions to *A Vision* in which he projected his System into the future before he finally decided to avoid the prophet's role and print none of them. In style, too, a particularly happy phrase would sometimes occur early and persist through many drafts while the context of the phrase changed out of all recognition.

A TYPICAL YEATS MANUSCRIPT seems on first examination to re-
semble the daw's nest Yeats described in "The Tower"; it appears to
be a jumble, a mere heap of confusion. If the work was of any length,
it would have been put together slowly. This means that the paper is
often of various sizes, the inks of various colors. Revisions in pencil
were always done with soft pencil in a very light stroke, so they are
now nearly indecipherable. Yeats's hand, in spite of the fact that it
was remarkably uniform, is very difficult to read. The writing, especially when intended for Yeats's eye alone, is in very rough state. The
spelling is atrocious.

My editing of the manuscripts of poems is conservative, though
I have not attempted to produce a diplomatic text. Jon Stallworthy
did attempt this when he printed manuscripts of Yeat's poems in
*Between the Lines,* and David Hayman has carried the effort even
further in *A First-Draft Version of Finnegans Wake.* I have not tried
to produce a diplomatic text of Yeats's manuscripts because I do not
think it can be done, and because such a text makes a reader's already
hard task even harder. Nothing that typography can do will actually
reproduce the peculiarities and difficulties of Yeats's manuscripts; even
photographic reproduction does not always do this very well because
of the varieties of inks used and the frequent intermixture of ink and
pencil.

In my editing I have expanded abbreviations and silently corrected
obvious misspellings, but I have not added any punctuation. I have
used the following devices in reproducing manuscripts of poems.
An × before a line means that Yeats has cancelled it; revisions within
a line are printed in cancelled type, as in this example:

~~Why dost thou brood~~   Linger no more where the fire burns bright

The original reading is followed immediately by the revised reading.
This practice is followed even when Yeats eventually abandoned the
whole line, cancellations and all. When alternate readings occur and
Yeats has allowed both of them to stand, they are printed in this way,
separating these readings with a slant sign:

For hands wave to them / are waving and eyes are a gleam.

Actually Yeats's revisions were written above and below as well as at the side of the words he first wrote. When lines of poetry are printed without normal spacing between them, this indicates that Yeats has tried various versions of a single line but has cancelled none of them. Whenever a line of verse reaches the form in which it was first printed, I place before it the number assigned to it in the *Variorum Edition*. Whenever I have been unable to decipher a word or group of words, I have indicated my failure and the length of the undeciphered passage. I have nowhere used the word "sic," and have tried to reduce to a minimum editorial queries indicating doubt of the accuracy of my reading. I have many doubts, but in the interests of a clean page use a query only when I cannot reduce Yeats's hieroglyph to any word which fits the context.

QUOTATIONS from published works by Yeats in copyright are made with the permission of Mrs. W. B. Yeats, Macmillan and Company Limited, The Macmillan Company, and A. P. Watt & Son: from *Autobiographies*, Macmillan and Company Limited, London, 1955: and from *Essays and Introductions* (copyright 1961 by Mrs. W. B. Yeats. Quotations from Yeats's manuscripts are made with the permission of Mrs. W. B. Yeats and A. P. Watt & Son.

My work on this book was done at the libraries of Harvard University (particularly Houghton and Widener), at the library of Trinity College, Dublin, at the National Library of Ireland, and at Burling Library, Grinnell College. I wish to acknowledge the unfailing kindness of the staff members of all these libraries, especially of the staff of the Houghton Library Reading Room, which is presided over by Shannon's portrait of Yeats.

My greatest debt is to Mrs. W. B. Yeats, who first in 1954–55 and again in the summer of 1960 made Yeats's manuscripts available to me, and who has placed no restrictions on my quotations from them. Next this is my debt to Sheldon P. Zitner, who encouraged my enterprise from the start, who has read the whole work twice and parts of it more often, and whose advice has been invaluable. The late Professor H. O. White of Trinity College, Dublin — "HO" to his innumerable friends — to whose memory I have dedicated this book, introduced me to Mrs. Yeats and never failed to be interested in and helpful to my work. Dublin cannot be the same without him. A Ford

Faculty Fellowship made possible my year in Dublin in 1954–55; a grant from the Lilly Endowment enabled me to return to Dublin in the summer of 1960.

C. B. B.

*Grinnell, Iowa*
*June 1964*

# CONTENTS

# YEATS
## *at work*

# AN INTRODUCTION

AMONG THE YEATS PAPERS IN DUBLIN are working or draft versions of a great many poems. The manuscripts of Yeats's earlier poems, up to the poems printed in The Green Helmet (1910), are usually late versions written into bound manuscript books. Few of the rough papers which preceded these versions seem to have survived. The situation is sometimes different with the poems Yeats wrote after 1908. From then on his rough papers were sometimes kept and filed, or he sometimes did all his work on a poem in a bound manuscript book. With many late poems it is possible to study the entire external process of composition, beginning with their prose sketches and continuing through successive drafts until Yeats corrects the final typescript. Chance more than any other factor seems to have governed what was kept and what thrown away.

From this material I have reproduced and analysed draft versions of the following poems: "The Hosting of the Sidhe" and "The Host of the Air," 1893; "The Lover asks Forgiveness because of his Many Moods," 1895; "Words," 1909; "The Wild Swans at Coole," 1916; "Nineteen Hundred and Nineteen"; section III of "The Tower," 1925; "Lullaby," 1929; "The Mother of God," 1931; section VIII of "Vacillation," 1932; "Ribh considers Christian Love insufficient," 1934; "The Gyres," 1937; "The Circus Animals' Desertion,"

1937–38. *This selection illustrates the normal process Yeats went through in composing poems. I have avoided on the one hand poems which Yeats largely composed in his head and then wrote down, such as "The Wheel," or poems which gave him particular trouble, such as "Parnell's Funeral." Yeats forced himself to write "Parnell's Funeral" at a time when he had not written a poem in over a year, using as his theme a passage from a lecture, "Modern Ireland," prepared for his last American lecture tour. When Yeats forced the creative process, for whatever reason, the work of composition was too long drawn out and complicated to be easily described.*

i

*Yeats almost always began work on a poem by composing what he called a "sketch" or "subject" in prose. These subjects state the content of the poems and note the principal images to be developed in them. They were often brief, though sometimes they were put through successive drafts. Some subjects are as long as the poems that grew out of them, some rough poems already. The subjects of section 1 of "The Tower" and of "Among School Children" are both short:*

What shall I do with this absurd toy which they have given me, this grotesque rattle? O heart, O nerves, you are as vigourous as ever. You still hunger for the whole world, and they have given you this toy.

Topic for poem. School children, and the thought that life will waste them, perhaps that no possible life can fulfill their own dreams or even their teacher's hope. Bring in the old thought that life prepares for what never happens.

[*Transcribed from a manuscript book begun at Oxford, April 7, 1921.*]

*Both these subjects, and indeed most others, show that while Yeats was actually composing poems they seldom worked out exactly as he had planned. The rattle became a kettle tied to a dog's tail in section 1 of "The Tower"; "Among School Children" loses its nostalgic tone during its course and becomes one of Yeats's most powerful statements of Unity of Being. The subject of "Among School Children" fails notably even to suggest the great poem that grew out of it.*

Yeats put the "Creed" which is the subject of "Under Ben Bulben" through three drafts. All three manuscripts are extremely difficult to read: the first, which is the longest, I was unable to transcribe; the second is a brief, summary version, perhaps the earliest of the three; the third draft, based directly on the first, went approximately as follows. (The title is taken from the head of the first draft.)

## CREED

I

I believe as did the old sages who sat under the palm trees, the banyan trees, or among the snowbound rocks, a thousand years before Christ was born; I believe as did the monks of the Mareotic Sea; as do country men who see the old fighting men and their fine women coming out of the mountain, moving from mountain to mountain.

II

And this is what I believe: that man stands between two eternities, that of his race, that of his soul. Further I declare that man serves these sword in hand and with an armoured mind. That only so armed does man pick the right mate, and only in the midst of a conflict which strains all his mind and his body, and to the utmost, has he wisdom enough to choose his right mate. The wisdom I seek is written on a sword, mirrored on a sword, on Sato's sword, a sword wrapped in a woman's old embroidery.

III

I declare that no evil can happen to the soul except from the soul — that death is a brief parting and brief sickness. What matter though the skies drop fire — children take hands and dance.

> [Transcribed from a late looseleaf manuscript notebook. This may be seen as Yeats left it in a microfilm copy at the Houghton Library. The materials in this notebook have now been distributed.]

The subject of "On Woman" anticipates the development of that poem very fully; that of "Lines Written in Dejection" is itself almost a poem [transcribed from the manuscript book begun Christmas, 1912]:

## SUBJECT FOR POEM

I give God praise for woman, what is a man's friendship worth beside hers? I praise God because she is a woman, and in her our minds and our bodies find rest. I praise first for her mind where she covers our vague thoughts with the substance of her revery, for Solomon grew wise in talking to her; and then for her body and the pleasure that comes with sleep; and because in her the vague desires of the dim sky meet the violent, and the curtain shivers: O God, grant me for my gift, not in this life for I begin to grow [old], but somewhere, that I shall love some woman so that every passion, pity, cruel desire, the affection that is full of tears, the abasement as before an image in a savage tent, hatred even it may be, shall find its prey. O God, it is a pity that even you cannot [grant] this to the old, in whom only the heart is insatiable.

> No longer the moon
> Sends me dark leopards
> Green eyed, and wavering [?] in the body
> Nor longer her white hares
> And that holy centaur of the hills
> And the young witches with lofty dissolute faces
> Now that I grow old
> I have nothing but the harsh sun
> I no longer climb in the white mountain valleys
> Our heroic mother the moon has vanished
> I am alone with the timid sun.

*It is difficult to state exactly the role played by these "subjects" in the total economy of poetic composition as Yeats practiced this, difficult because the relations of subjects to finished poems differ greatly. The physical process of working out a poem through successive drafts usually began with these subjects, but it is clear that before writing the subject Yeats had carried the internal, mental aspect of composition much further with some poems than with others. The subjects of "Among School Children" and "Byzantium" illustrate extremes of preparation and lack of preparation. After writing the subject of "Among School Children" Yeats still had nearly everything to do: the poem's principal themes are not anticipated in the subject, among the correlatives used in the poem only the children and the schoolroom setting have been chosen.*

In the subject of "Byzantium," on the contrary, the materials of the poem are almost all assembled, and are with one exception in the order in which they appear in the finished poem.

Describe Byzantium as it is in the system towards the end of the first Christian millennium. A walking mummy; flames at the street corners where the soul is purified. Birds of hammered gold singing in the golden trees. In the harbour [dolphins] offering their backs to the wailing dead that they may carry them to paradise.

[*Transcribed from the* MS. *of the 1930 Diary.*]

The question cannot be fully answered until all surviving "subjects of poems" by Yeats are collected and studied, including "subjects for poems" — and there are many such — which never developed into poems. Meanwhile here are some tentative conclusions based on such subjects as I have studied: (1) Yeats wrote subjects at various stages of his thinking about a poem; sometimes he had the poem rather fully formed in his mind, at other times he was only beginning to plan it. (2) A close relation of finished poem to subject does not indicate that Yeats found the actual writing of the poem easy. The subjects of "Coole Park, 1929" and "Byzantium" rather fully anticipate the poems that grew out of them. Jon Stallworthy has shown that Yeats had extreme difficulty composing "Coole Park, 1929"; in writing "Byzantium," as I have shown elsewhere,[1] his whole attack shows complete mastery of his ideas and of his technique. (3) Such subjects as I have studied do not by themselves indicate whether Yeats is recording a major or a minor inspiration; they do not even hint at the greatness or lack of greatness of the poems that will grow out of them. Until a full study is made we shall have to be content to conclude that these subjects were for Yeats a necessary beginning. Soon after composing a subject, at times on the same day, Yeats would start work on the poem.

ii

Once he had written his subjects, Yeats had "to find for them some natural speech, rhythm and syntax, and to set it out in some pattern, so seeming old that it may seem all men's speech" ("The Bounty of Sweden" — 1925). This involved great labor of which Yeats often complained. He had to develop a form suited to his particular subject, he had to find and invent descriptive detail and correlatives that would put flesh on its bare bones, and he had — hardest of all — to make "some natural speech." He accomplished this in stages when his poem was at all complex; in some short poems he seems to do everything at once. He always, I think, worked on the whole poem though sometimes he started in the middle or even at the end; he did not try to finish one part of it before moving on to the next. Sometimes he wrote drafts not governed by his intended form; these are always, I think, very early. Then he wrote a series of early drafts where everything he does is, after some experimenting, governed by the chosen pattern of line length and rhyme scheme. Then in intermediate drafts Yeats would assemble his whole poems; if these pleased him at all he would initial or sign them. He often made clean copies of such intermediate drafts so that his typist could transcribe them. Yeats then went to work on these transcriptions; he would improve his phrasing, make subtle metrical adjustments, and systematically punctuate his poem. Very often in these transcriptions various parts of a poem are in various stages of finish. When Yeats detected a bad spot, he would make further manuscript drafts until he had got the poem right. He carried on the process of revision in his proofs, and even after printing.

Yeats sometimes made drafts for parts of poems before he had decided on the form of the poem. Yeats probably wrote many such drafts, but very few have survived. Such as have survived are among his most interesting and tantalizing manuscripts; interesting because they record the earliest stages of Yeats at work, tantalizing because they are almost impossible to read. One draft of this sort has been printed three times, that of the first stanza of "Sailing to Byzantium." [2] I print below an early draft of what is now stanza v of "Among School Children" as another illustration of what Yeats did in the early stages of forming a poem. Yeats began work on stanza v of "Among School Children," perhaps on the whole poem, in this manuscript: [3]

| | | | |
|---|---|---|---|
| lap | fears | | *lap* |
| shape | ~~tears~~ | | made |
| | ~~years~~ | | *escape* |
| | ~~forth~~ | birth | betrayed |
| | forth | | shape |
| | | | head |

✕ What mother of a child shrieking the first scream
✕ Of a soul

Of a soul struggling to leave
✕ Degradation of the [word undeciphered]
✕ Still knowing that it is betrayed [?]
Still half remembering that it [is] betrayed

What mother with a child upon her breast
Shedding there its tears, all the despair
Of the soul betrayed into the flesh
Would think — [if] it came before her in a vision
~~The image~~   What the child would be at sixty years
A compensation for the

[There are some other jottings on this page which I cannot transcribe.]

Here the lines Yeats drafts are not governed by the stanza form
of "Among School Children," his adaptation of ottava rima. This
was Yeats's favorite eight-line stanza, and he used it for many of his
most famous meditative and philosophic poems. Since almost the
first thing Yeats did when starting to work on a poem was to establish his form, a practice illustrated by most of the manuscripts I
reproduce, the fact that he had not chosen his form is a fairly certain
indication that Yeats began "Among School Children" with what
is now stanza v. It seems hardly possible that were he past the mid-
point in composing the finished poem he would draft a stanza not
governed by form.

There are other bits of evidence that Yeats began "Among School
Children" with stanza v, these external. Shortly before writing out
the "topic" from which the poem developed (already quoted),
Yeats made this entry in the same manuscript book:

I think of my grandfather and grandmother, to whom I was so much,
and as I look in the glass, as I look at old age coming, I wonder if they
would [have] thought it worth the bother. What have I that they
value? I think of my father and mother, and of my first coming to
their house. What have I that they value, what would have seemed
sufficient at the moment? My thoughts would have seemed super-
stition to the one and to the other a denial of God.

This is essentially the thought expressed in stanza v of the poem, which repeats one of Yeats's most repelling ideas, a young mother's prevision of her infant son as an old man, expressed earlier in the second stanza of the song that opens At the Hawk's Well. Here as so often with Yeats a new poem uses material found in an already finished poem. In stanza v of "Among School Children" it is content, not form, that governs the draft lines Yeats writes, though if we combine the last two words from the list of rhyme words in the middle of the manuscript page with the list on the right they point clearly to an ottava rima rhyme scheme and include all the rhyme words in the finished stanza except "decide." Choosing his rhyme words or rhyme sounds was a standard practice with Yeats when blocking out a stanza.

I reconstruct the order in which Yeats wrote the material on this manuscript page as follows: First he wrote the list of rhyme words in the center of the page which ends with the rhyme words of his closing couplet (birth, forth) carefully reversed from the order in which he originally wrote them down. Then I think he invented the fine couplet:

A compensation for the pang of his birth
Or the uncertainty of his setting forth.

Perhaps he wrote this down someplace else or was trusting his memory, for here he merely dubs it in by writing "A compensation for the." In the draft lines found on this page Yeats was trying to invent matter that might introduce this couplet and fill out his stanza. Yeats then went back to the top of the page and wrote the list of rhyme words to the right. This includes enough of the controlling words of the stanza to indicate that it was now rapidly shaping up in his mind.

A draft of stanza v from a manuscript of the whole poem finished June 14, 1926, makes it almost certain that Yeats worked with the above sheet of notes before him, for as we move back and forth from notes to draft we find that in the draft Yeats further explores nearly every detail found in the notes: the child's cries, its struggle to escape the degradation of incarnation, its recollections of immortality. Yeats slowly discards details that do not work as he finds the details he needs to fill out his stanza.

5
What youthful mother, rocking on her lap
X  A fretful thing that knows itself betrayed
X  And struggles with vain clamour to escape
X  Before its memory and apprehension fade
X  Before ~~its~~   the memories of its freedom fade
X  Would think — had she ~~foreknown~~  foreknowledge of that shape
X  Would think her son could she foreknow that shape
X  Her son with sixty winters on his head
X  With maybe sixty winter ~~on~~   upon his head
X  With sixty or more winters upon his head

[*The next twelve lines were written on the facing page.*]

   A thing, the ~~oblivious honey has~~   generative honey had betrayed
X  And that shrieks out and struggles to escape
35 And that must sleep, ~~or~~   shriek struggle to escape
X  As its drugged memories gleam or fade
X  As it
X  As still but half drugged memories decide
X  As its drugged memories may decide
X  Where some brief memories or the drug decide
X  ~~As flitting~~   As sudden memories or the drug decide
36 As recollection or the drug decide
37 Would think her son, ~~could she foreknow~~   did she but see that
        shape
38 With sixty or more winters on ~~his~~   its head

[*Returns to the principal draft.*]

39 A compensation for the pang of his birth
40 Or the uncertainty of his setting forth? [4]

Many early drafts controlled by a form Yeats had invented or was
soon to invent have survived, though often they represent only parts
of a poem. Apparently Yeats normally started without a fully set
form. Indeed in only one manuscript known to me ("Byzantium")
does Yeats set his rhyme scheme at the top of his first draft. Charac-
teristically he feels his way into the form by experimenting with
rhyme schemes and, especially, line lengths. In the early drafts of

section III of "The Tower" we will find Yeats trying lines with three or four stresses before deciding on three; in early drafts of "Lullaby" and "The Gyres" the stanza form emerges, so to speak. But the first thing Yeats did was to set his form; once he had set it he rarely changed. Rhyme words and rhyme sounds were also established very early in the process of composing and they will often stand firm while the entire context changes around them. They are abandoned only when Yeats has decided that a radical new beginning is needed to remove a bad spot from a poem.

In these early drafts Yeats slowly accumulates additional correlatives, that is the descriptive detail, objects, and images he needs to express the idea contained in his subject. With these change is constant; they come into a poem and go out of it through a long process during which Yeats will finally select those details that best serve his purpose. The multiple drafts of lines 9–32 of "Nineteen Hundred and Nineteen" illustrate this refinement. As this process is going on Yeats will slowly — sometimes with agonizing slowness — find the words he wants, find that "natural speech so seeming old that it may seem all men's speech." The early drafts of "The Wild Swans at Coole" brilliantly illustrate this slow improvement of Yeats's diction.

Most of the surviving manuscripts of Yeats's poems are intermediate drafts, drafts that is of whole poems which are very often initialed or signed, and dated. (Incidentally, these are usually the dates given by Richard Ellmann and others for the composition of particular poems; Yeats rarely recorded the dates on which he actually finished a poem. Often many months elapsed between intermediate and final drafts.) These are always working drafts in which Yeats constantly revises as he goes along. In most intermediate drafts the various parts of the poem show various states of finish. There is no pattern I can discover in the occurrence of bad spots in particular poems. The first two stanzas of "Sailing to Byzantium" had to be rewritten; stanzas 2 and 3 of part 1 of "Nineteen Hundred and Nineteen"; the last stanza of "The Circus Animals' Desertion." These intermediate drafts are fully illustrated in the discussion of particular poems which follows. Very often Yeats made a clean copy of such intermediate drafts so that a typist could transcribe it.

Yeats's poems were typed at this point, usually in multiple copies. Yeats preferred to have Mrs. Yeats transcribe his manuscripts, but whether she or another made the typed versions, great care was taken not to add anything, particularly not to add any punctuation. When Yeats went to work on a typescript, he would first of all correct it, filling in blanks which the typist had left when unable to read his writing, improving spelling and capitalization. He would make careful adjustments of meter by dropping or adding syllables, usually one syllable words. Yeats's manuscripts are very lightly punctuated, and he often used one copy of a typescript solely for punctuation. A typescript of "News for the Delphic Oracle" with the punctuation Yeats added inserted in brackets illustrates this practice.

## NEWS FOR THE DELPHIC ORACLE

### I

There all the golden codgers lay[,]
There the silver dew[,]
And the great water sighed for love
And the wind sighed too[.]
Man-picker Niamh leant and sighed
By Oisin on the grass[;]
There sighed amid his choir of love
Tall Pythagoras.
Plotinus came and looked about[,]
The salt flakes on his breast[,]
And having stretched and yawned awhile
Lay sighing like the rest.

### II

Straddling each a dolphin's back
And steadied by a fin
The Holy Innocents re-live their death[,]
Their wounds open again[.]
The ecstatic waters laugh because
Those cries are sweet and strange[,]
Through their ancestral patterns dance
And the brute dolphins plunge
Until in some cliff-sheltered bay
Where wades the choir of love
Proffering its sacred laurel crowns[,]
They pitch their burdens off.

III

Slim adolescence that a nymph has stripped[,]
Peleus on Thetis stares[,]
Her limbs are delicate as an eyelid[,]
Love has blinded him with tears[;]
But Thetis' belly listens[.]
Down the mountain walls
From where Pan's cavern is
Intolerable music falls[.]
Foul goathead, brutal arm appear,
Belly, shoulder, bum
Flash fishlike[;] nymphs and satyrs
Copulate in the foam.

*This is an excellent example of rhetorical as opposed to grammatical punctuation; it suggests to us, if we remember that in his own readings Yeats always paused at line ends whether there was a mark of punctuation or not, how Yeats heard the poem and how he wanted us to hear it.*[5]

*If Yeats became seriously dissatisfied with some section of a poem that had already been typed, he would usually start work on the offending lines in the margins and between the lines of typing. When he had used up the available space, he would begin again in manuscript. This process is illustrated below in the drafts of "Nineteen Hundred and Nineteen" and "The Circus Animals' Desertion." These new manuscripts were in their turn typed and corrected until Yeats was satisfied with a poem. A final typescript was made from which the poem was printed. Yeats continued correction in proof, though in later years he made few changes. Even this was not the end, for Yeats continued to improve his poems after he had had them printed; he used successive editions for such improvement. Here again in his later years his practice grew more conservative. Readers of the Macmillan Wild Swans (1919), Michael Robartes (in Later Poems, 1922), The Tower (1928), The Winding Stair (1933), and A Full Moon in March (1935) generally found the final versions in these books.*

### iii

Yeats's revisions move in three directions, though the third is not operative in his early poetry. The first is toward correctness, toward an effort to make a poem in process, say a ballad such as "The Hosting of the Sidhe," conform more fully with Yeats's abstract ideal or norm of what a ballad should be. A second type of revision, which might be called mimesis or imitation — though given the long history of these words in literary criticism one would like to find a fresh word — involves an effort to make the imagined scene or action of a poem increasingly vivid sensuously. Both types of revision involve primarily meter and diction, both are illustrated in the revisions of "The Hosting of the Sidhe" and "The Host of the Air." A third type of revision is concerned with the management of the personae invented or being invented for a particular poem; such revisions demonstrate Yeats's effort to control the expressiveness of these personae, to properly modulate the voice speaking the poem.

The personae of most of Yeats's early poems are so vague and abstract that they have almost been refined out of existence. And herein, I think, we find one source of the limitation of Yeats's poetry up through The Wind Among the Reeds. The vagueness and abstractness of the personae of Yeats's early poems will be discussed in the following chapter. Here it is enough to say that because Yeats often failed to define sharply the personae of his early poems his revisions of them are two dimensional only, involve what we have called correctness and mimesis. But singsong, however subtle and refined it may become, is good only in limited contexts, and realism is not the goal of a lyric poet.

Wordsworth defined the poet as a man speaking to men, and, however much Yeats disliked Wordsworth's moralizing and didacticism, he came fully to agree with his definition of a poet. Yeats came into his own as a poet when he developed and then made operative a belief that a poem must be a personal utterance, though the phrase "personal utterance" may easily mislead us unless we define it by observing how it worked in Yeats's own poetry and the various ways in which he qualified it by later observations, as in his description of an effective poetic persona in "The First Principle" quoted below. Certainly Yeats at no time in his life regarded poetry as a mode of what is loosely called "self expression"; the very complexity of his concept of the self as involving the "mask" and the "anti-self" make us sure of this. And in the same essay from which "The First Principal" is quoted Yeats wrote "I knew . . . that I must turn from that modern literature Jonathan Swift compared to the web a spider draws out of its bowels; I hated and still hate with an ever growing hatred the literature of the point of view."

Still Yeats did believe that the voice of a poet is the voice of a man, that this must be so because poetry is memorable speech and speech comes from a man. Beginning with "Adam's Curse" most of Yeats's poems are personal utterances, and because they are Yeats is constantly involved in managing the personae he has invented to speak them. This is particularly true of poems using an I-persona. This is Yeats's favorite; sixty-two of Yeats's poems begin with the word "I" to count those instances alone. Much of Yeats's revision of his later poetry is concerned with developing and controlling the expressiveness of his personae. Such revisions are both more important and more revealing than revisions made in the interests of correctness and mimesis. Three dimensional revision will be found at work in the successive drafts of "The Wild Swans at Coole."

Yeats stated his concept of an effective persona far better than I can state it in the opening sentences of "A General Introduction for My Work" written in 1937 and recently printed for the first time in Essays and Introductions. He called this part of his essay "The First Principle":

A poet writes always of his personal life, in his finest work out of its tragedy, whatever it be, remorse, lost love, or mere loneliness; he never speaks directly as to someone at the breakfast table, there is always a phantasmagoria. . . . Even when the poet seems most himself, when he is Raleigh and gives potentates the lie, or Shelley 'a nerve o'er which do creep the else unfelt oppressions of this earth,' or Byron when 'the soul wears out the breast' as 'the sword outwears its sheath,' he is never the bundle of accident and incoherence that sits down to breakfast; he has been reborn as an idea, something intended, complete. A novelist might describe his accidence, his incoherence, he must not; he is more type than man, more passion than type. He is Lear, Romeo, Oedipus, Tiresias; he has stepped out of a play, and even the woman he loves is Rosalind, Cleopatra, never The Dark Lady. He is part of his own phantasmagoria and we adore him because nature has grown intelligible, and by so doing a part of our creative power.

Yeats sometimes had difficulty achieving this ideal; there is always a danger when using an I-persona that too much of his accidence will creep into a poem, and we will find that this indeed happened in early drafts of many of the poems studied below. Yeats's principal problem in revision was then to control this accidence. This was particularly difficult when the persona was Yeats himself, for Yeats had then to invent a phantasmagoric Yeats, had to refine the accidence of a particular man involved in an actual situation in the alembic of his imagination. Perhaps the greatest paradox in Yeats's development as a poet was that he became truly a public poet only after he had become a private one; eventually he came to express whatever was nearest to hand, say a statuette carved in lapis lazuli standing on the mantel in his study, in the mode of public speech for which he has so justly been praised.

Eight of the later poems studied use variations of the I-persona, though sometimes only incidentally: "Words," "The Wild Swans at Coole," "Nineteen Hundred and Nineteen," section III of "The Tower," section VIII of "Vacillation," "Ribh considers Christian Love insufficient," "The Gyres," and "The Circus Animals' Desertion." In "Words," "Vacillation," "Ribh considers Christian Love insufficient," and "The Gyres" Yeats had little or no trouble managing his personae, and it is, I think, because their personae came right from the start that Yeats appears to have written these poems with relative ease. In the others Yeats had trouble managing the personae, sometimes serious trouble. When the trouble is serious Yeats will write draft after draft until he has transmuted accidence into permanence. In "Lullaby" and "The Mother of God" Yeats invents more objective personae, the mother who speaks the lullaby, and Mary. But even in these poems Yeats's belief that a poem should be in some way a personal utterance controls what Yeats writes, indeed enables him in the later poem to use material he might not otherwise have managed.

*1*

# POEMS FROM
# The Wind Among the Reeds

THE earliest bound manuscript book preserved among the Yeats papers in Dublin is inscribed "W. B. Yeats. August 29th. 1893." It contains draft and final versions of many of the poems Yeats published in *The Wind Among the Reeds*, along with others which he printed but never collected and some which have never been printed. There are several lists of poems, in which Yeats explores the order of poems to be included in *The Wind Among the Reeds*, and partial working drafts of *The Shadowy Waters* (1900). The latest date in the book is December 1895. This manuscript book is particularly interesting because it contains love poems addressed to both Maud Gonne and Diana Vernon: the uncollected poem "The Glove and the Cloak" (poem jj in the *Variorum Edition*) obviously refers to Maud Gonne; "The Lover asks Forgiveness because of his Many Moods" is just as obviously about Diana Vernon. Manuscripts of both poems occur in this book.

*i*

## "The Hosting of the Sidhe"

YEATS TRIED TO RESERVE his bound manuscript books for clean copies of poems he had finished or nearly finished, but very often in the process of copying out a poem he would start revising it, sometimes going on to successive revised versions. I believe that the 1893 manuscript book was used in this way, and doubt if it records the earliest versions of any of the poems included in it. The three poems chosen for study are among the most revised poems in the book. Yeats has numbered the pages of the book; three successive versions of "The Hosting of the Sidhe" are found on pages 1–6:

1

They call from the cairn on Knocknarea
They are calling calling from Knocknarea

They call from the grave of Clooth-na-Bare
And the ~~water~~   pool that is over Clooth-na-Bare

Caolte tosses his burning hair

But Niam murmurs 'away come away'

2

'~~Why dost thou brood~~   Linger no more where the fire burns bright
6  Filling thy heart with a mortal dream
~~White~~   ~~Our~~   ~~Her~~   For hands wave to them/ are waving and
      eyes ~~are~~  a gleam
8  ~~To draw it away~~   Away, come away to the dim twilight'

3

White arms glimmer and red lips are apart
If any man gaze on the Danaan band
They come between him and the deed of his hand
They come between him and the hope of his heart

4

✕  But some afar on their way
Ah somewhere afar on their ringing way
— No hope or deed was a whit so fair —
And no hope or deed is a whit so fair
And the world has not hope or deed/ deed or hope ~~so~~   as fair
Caolte tosses his burning hair
But Niam murmurs
                          'Away come away'
                          August 29th [1893]

Yeats first dated the next draft August 29th, then cancelled 29 and
wrote 30 above it.

> They are calling calling from Knocknarea
> They rush from the cairn of Knocknarea
> To the pool

×   They call and they rush from Knock etc

> And the pool that is over Clooth-na-Bare
>
> Caolte tosses his burning hair
>
> But Niam murmurs 'away come away'
>
> 'Linger no more where the fire is bright
>
> 6  Filling thy heart with a mortal dream
>
> For hands are waving and eyes ~~are bright~~   a-gleam
> For our breasts are heaving our eyes a-gleam
>
> 8  Away come away to the dim twilight'
>
> 'Our white breasts heave and our red lips part;
> Our ~~arms~~   white arms wave and our red lips part
>
> If any man gaze on our ~~ringing~~   rushing band
>
> 11  We come between him and the deed of his hand
>
> 12  We come between him and the hope of his heart'
>
> They are rushing by on their ringing way
>
> And there is not a hope nor deed as fair;
>
> Caolte tosses his burning hair
>
> But Niam whispers 'away come away'

In the third version Yeats gets closer to the wording of the poem as it
was first printed in *The National Observer* on October 7, 1893.

> The host is calling from Knocknarea
>
> And the pool that is over Clooth-na-Bare
>
> Caolte tosses his burning hair
>
> But Niam murmurs 'Away come away'

*

> 'Linger no more where the fire is bright
> 6  Filling thy heart with a mortal dream

For our breasts are heaving ~~our~~   and eyes agleam
8 Away come away to the dim twilight

*

~~Our~~   And arms are waving our lips apart
10 And if a ~~man~~   any gaze on our rushing band
11 We come between him and the deed of his hand
12 We come between him and the hope of his heart.

*

13 The host ~~rushes by~~   is rushing twixt night and day,
~~And~~   There is not a hope nor a ~~dream~~   deed as fair,
Caolte tosses his burning hair
But Niam murmurs
'Away come away'

Apparently Yeats had done the rough work on this poem before copying it into his manuscript book, for his stanza form and rhyme scheme have been determined, as well as his allusions to Knocknarea, Clooth-na-Bare, Caolte, and Niam. In these drafts Yeats is working for correctness and a more vivid imitation of the imagined scene, a process which he continued in printed versions of the poem until it reached final form in *The Wind Among the Reeds*. To help us see just what Yeats did with this poem by revising it, the successive versions of each line are assembled below, beginning with the earliest MS. and ending with the text found in *The Wind Among the Reeds*. (Manuscripts are designated "MS. 1," "MS. 2," "MS. 3." Printed versions are given the designations found in the *Variorum Edition*. NO stands for *The National Observer*, October 7, 1893; 7 for *The Celtic Twilight*, published December, 1893; 11 for *The Wind Among the Reeds*. I have ignored typographical changes, and changes in punctuation at the ends of lines.)

1 They call from the cairn on Knocknarea   MS. 1
They are calling calling from Knocknarea   MSS. 1 and 2
They rush from the cairn of Knocknarea   MS. 2
They call and they rush from Knocknarea   MS. 2
The host is calling from Knocknarea   MS. 3
The host is riding from Knocknarea   NO, 7, 11

2 They call from the grave of Clooth-na-Bare   MS. 1
And the pool that is over Clooth-na-Bare   MSS. 1, 2, and 3
And over the grave of Clooth-na-Bare   NO, 7, 11

3 Caolte tosses his burning hair   MSS. 1, 2, and 3
Caolte tossing his burning hair   NO, 7, 11

4 But Niam murmurs 'away come away'   MSS. 1, 2, and 3
And Niam calling, 'away, come away   NO, 7, 11

5 Linger no more where the fire burns bright   MS. 1
Linger no more where the fire is bright   MSS. 2 and 3
And brood no more where the fire is bright   NO, 7
Empty your heart of its mortal dream   11

6 Filling thy heart with a mortal dream   MSS. 1, 2, 3; NO, 7
The winds awaken, the leaves whirl round   11

7 For hands are waving and eyes agleam   MSS. 1 and 2
For our breasts are heaving our eyes a-gleam   MS. 2
For our breasts are heaving and eyes a-gleam   MS. 3
For breasts are heaving and eyes a-gleam   NO, 7
Our cheeks are pale, our hair is unbound   11

8 Away, come away to the dim twilight   MSS. 1, 2, 3; NO, 7
Our breasts are heaving, our eyes are agleam   11

9 White arms glimmer and red lips are apart   MS. 1
Our white breasts heave and our red lips part   MS. 2
Our white arms wave and our red lips part   MS. 2
And arms are waving our lips apart   MS. 3
Arms are a-waving and lips apart   NO, 7
Our arms are waving, our lips are apart   11

10 If any man gaze on the Dan'aan band   MS. 1
If any man gaze on our rushing band   MS. 2
And if any gaze on our rushing band   MS. 3; NO, 7, 11

11 They come between him and the deed of his hand   MS. 1
We come between him and the deed of his hand
                                MSS. 2 and 3; NO, 7, 11

12 They come between him and the hope of his heart   MS. 1
We come between him and the hope of his heart
                                MSS. 2 and 3; NO, 7, 11

13  Ah somewhere afar on their ringing way   MS. 1
    They are rushing by on their ringing way   MS. 2
    The host is rushing twixt night and day   MS. 3; NO, 7, 11

14  — No hope or deed was a whit so fair —   MS. 1
    And no hope or deed is a whit so fair   MS. 1
    And the world has not hope or deed as fair   MS. 1
    And there is not a hope nor deed as fair   MS. 2
    There is not a hope nor a deed as fair   MS. 3
    And where is there hope or deed as fair   NO, 7, 11

15  Caolte tosses his burning hair   MSS. 1, 2, and 3
    Caolte tossing his burning hair   NO, 7, 11

16  But Niam murmurs 'Away come away'   MS. 1
    But Niam whispers 'Away come away'   MS. 2
    But Niam murmurs 'Away come away'   MS. 3
    And Niam calling 'Away come away'   NO, 7, 11

This run of drafts is a simple but characteristic illustration of what Yeats accomplished when he revised his poems. By revision Yeats increased the degree of energy both within the single lines and among the lines that constitute a verse unit — here a four-line stanza rhymed abba. I think his revisions always achieved this result; though I sometimes feel that Yeats carried some detail of a revision beyond the point where he achieved the best expression, I have never felt that revision has failed to improve a poem as a whole. As for diction and phrasing, Yeats, early and late, worked hard to achieve Swift's ideal — "Proper words in proper places." He sought at once to find the inevitable word, and to arrange these words according to a syntax based on the spoken language. The finished version of "The Hosting of the Sidhe" is both more energetic and more colloquial than the drafts. Finally, we observe that Yeats finished his poem a part at a time: lines 1–4 and 14–16 in *The National Observer*, lines 5–9 in *The Wind Among the Reeds*, lines 10–13 in manuscripts 2 and 3. Again, this is typical.

I have divided my commentary on the details of Yeats's revisions into units corresponding to the stanzas. In the manuscripts and in the two earliest printings of the poem the stanzas are separated; in the finished poem they are printed without breaks.

LINES 1–4.   Here Yeats's principal revisions affect his verbs; they involve both the form of his verbs and the content. Yeats shifts from the present tense to the progressive present — the progressive present dominates the finished poem — while moving toward increased energy of statement. Yeats tries two forms of lines 1–2 in MS. 1:

> They call from the cairn on Knocknarea
> They call from the grave of Clooth-na-Bare

and

> They are calling calling from Knocknarea
> And the pool that is over Clooth-na-Bare

The repetition of "They call from" is at once too easy and too static, so Yeats introduces the progressive present "are calling," doubling the participle in line 1 and dropping it from line 2. There has been some gain in energy, but the solution is still too easy. In MS. 2 Yeats tries two solutions: "They rush from the cairn of Knocknarea/ To the pool" and "They call and they rush from Knocknarea/ To the pool." At this point Yeats perhaps realized that he was involved in a double difficulty; he has been using the pronoun "they" without an antecedent with the result that when his reader gets to the names Caolte and Niam in lines 3–4 he will assume that "they" refers to them, "call" and "rush" do not combine happily because they are necessarily unsimultaneous. In MS. 3 Yeats solves the first problem by introducing the noun "host" in place of the pronoun "they":

> The host is calling from Knocknarea
> And the pool that is over Clooth-na-Bare

Eventually this reading will supply the titles, successively "The Faery Host," "The Host," and "The Hosting of the Sidhe," and meanwhile the poem moves better when first the "host" and then two individuals from that host, Caolte and Niam, summon mortals to join the Sidhe. But "calling" is still static; the movement involved in the cancelled word "rush" has been lost, and now Yeats merely summons us to join the Sidhe on Knocknarea. Before Yeats printed the poem in *The National Observer*, he completed the procession image with which the poem now begins:

> The host is riding from Knocknarea
> And over the grave of Clooth-na-Bare.

While all this change was going on in lines 1–2, lines 3–4 remained untouched until Yeats revised his poem for *The National Observer*:

Caolte tosses his burning hair
But Niam murmurs 'away come away.'

Yeats finished stanza 1 when he changed his verbs to the progressive present and transferred the summons from the host to Niam:

Caolte tossing his burning hair
And Niam calling, 'away, come away.'

LINES 5–8.   Yeats's revision of stanza 2 was radical, but far less compli-cated. The stanza remained fairly stable through its second printing in *The Celtic Twilight*; then Yeats rewrote it for *The Wind Among the Reeds*. In this rewriting he replaced lines 5 and 8 by new lines which he put into the middle of his stanza (as lines 6 and 7); he revised his old lines 6 and 7 and transposed them so that they now provide his "a" rhymes at the beginning and end of the stanza:

And brood no more where the fire is bright
Filling thy heart with a mortal dream,
For our breasts are heaving and eyes a-gleam;
Away, come away to the dim twilight.

Empty your heart of its mortal dream.
The winds awaken, the leaves whirl round,
Our cheeks are pale, our hair is unbound,
Our breasts are heaving, our eyes are agleam,

Perhaps Yeats made these changes partly because of the sheer weak-ness and emptiness of the lines he abandoned; line 8 in the original version was particularly weak and empty. Certainly Yeats's new lines are far more energetic than his old; the whirling leaves are particularly interesting because they adumbrate the gyre of Yeats's later poetry. Another possible explanation, and here I am on surer ground, is that the changes are involved with Yeats's decision to abandon the separa-tion of his stanzas. It would not have been enough merely to shove together the successive stanzas, keeping a full stop at the end of every fourth line; some enjambments are needed. Yeats provided a forced enjambment, so to speak, at line 4 when he replaced a period with a colon; by the revision described above he provided a true enjambment here at line 8. He increased the force of this enjambment by his revision of line 9.

LINES 9–12. Yeats did most of his revising of these lines in manuscript. The development of line 9 is complicated by the fact that Yeats decided while working on MS. 2 to rearrange some of his descriptive detail. The "heaving breasts" of the revised ninth line he put into stanza 2, the "waving hands" of the original seventh line he brought down into stanza 3. During the transposition "white breasts heave" became "breasts are heaving." Perhaps this is an example of Yeats's timidity in handling details involving sexual attraction in *The Wind Among the Reeds,* a timidity certainly illustrated in his revision of "The Lover asks Forgiveness," discussed below. "White arms" are less suggestive than "white breasts." Yeats revised the line again in MS. 3, getting rid of the eight low words that had crept into it and changing "wave" to the progressive present "waving." The line now read "And arms are waving our lips apart," which without punctuation seems rather silly. Before printing the poem in *The National Observer* Yeats dropped the initial "and"; he also invented the awkward form "a-waving" to replace the syllable lost at the beginning of the line. Revisions like this one are frequent in Yeats's later poetry. Their result is to begin a line with a strong accent, and with an important word. When Yeats revised the line for *The Wind Among the Reeds,* he got rid of "a-waving" and cast the line in its final form. In the successive versions of this line we observe again continually increasing energy and movement. Here Yeats moved from "White arms glimmer and red lips are apart" of MS. 1 to "Our arms are waving, our lips are apart." The rest of the stanza caused less trouble, though the revisions made have the important effect of changing the point of view. In MS. 1 we are observing the host of the Sidhe from the outside:

> If any man gaze on the Danaan band
> They come between him and the deed of his hand
> They come between him and the hope of his heart.

When Yeats finishes these lines in MS. 3, we are part of the host:

> And if any gaze on our rushing band
> We come between him and the deed of his hand
> We come between him and the hope of his heart.

The change from "Danaan band" to "rushing band" shows what revision of a single word can accomplish. The exotic word "Danaan" will puzzle most readers, thereby interrupting their experience of the poem; it is also static, whereas the participle "rushing" sustains the image of the riding host.

LINES 13–16.  Since stanza 4 largely echoes stanza 1 in its development — the echo of the rhyme sounds is exact — most of the changes made in four follow from the changes already made in one. When, for example, Yeats in MS. 3 changed line 1 to read "The host is calling from Knocknarea" he also changed line 13 to read "The host is rushing twixt night and day"; when in *The National Observer* he changed lines 3 and 4 to read "Caolte tossing" and "Niam calling" he made the same changes in lines 15 and 16. During the process of revision Yeats noticeably increased the similarity of stanzas 1 and 4; they are far more alike in the finished poem than in MS. 1. Only the complex revision of line 14 is not explained by Yeats's endeavor to make the echo of stanza 1 more exact. From MS. 1 on Yeats uses line 14 to pick up the thought of stanza 3 by repeating the words "hope" and "deed," uses it, that is, to express again the attraction of the invitation to join the faery host. While revising this line Yeats shifts from direct statement of the contrast between our world and faeryland ("And the world has not deed or hope as fair"), to an implied statement of the contrast ("There is not a hope nor a deed as fair"), to a question ("And where is there hope or deed as fair"); his expression of the attraction of faeryland grows increasingly subtle, increasingly tantalizing.

The total effect of Yeats's revision can be judged best when MS. 1 and the finished poem are put side by side; indeed the great effect of his typographical revision can be judged only when the two versions are brought together.

1

They are calling calling from Knocknarea
And the pool that is over Clooth-na-Bare
Caolte tosses his burning hair
But Niam murmurs 'away come away'

2

'Linger no more where the fire burns bright
Filling thy heart with a mortal dream
For hands are waving and eyes a gleam
Away, come away to the dim twilight'

3

White arms glimmer and red lips are apart
If any man gaze on the Danaan band
They come between him and the deed of his hand
They come between him and the hope of his heart

4

Ah somewhere afar on their ringing way
And the world has not deed or hope as fair
Caolte tosses his burning hair
But Niam murmurs
                'Away come away'

## THE HOSTING OF THE SIDHE

The host is riding from Knocknarea
And over the grave of Clooth-na-Bare;
Caoilte tossing his burning hair,
And Niamh calling *Away, come away:*
*Empty your heart of its mortal dream.*
*The winds awaken, the leaves whirl round,*
*Our cheeks are pale, our hair is unbound,*
*Our breasts are heaving, our eyes are agleam,*
*Our arms are waving, our lips are apart;*
*And if any gaze on our rushing band,*
*We come between him and the deed of his hand,*
*We come between him and the hope of his heart.*
The host is rushing 'twixt night and day,
And where is there hope or deed as fair?
Caoilte tossing his burning hair,
And Niamh calling *Away, come away.*

*ii*

## "The Host of the Air"

YEATS WROTE "The Host of the Air" while he was working on
*The Land of Heart's Desire* (1894). Both poem and play exploit the

theme of the mortal woman who leaves her husband to join the Sidhe. This theme attracted Yeats because it seemed to him to express his relations with Maud Gonne: in section XXIV of the manuscript "First Draft" of Yeats's *Autobiographies* he says, "I began to write *The Land of Heart's Desire* . . . and put into it my own despair. I could not tell why Maud Gonne had turned from me unless she had done so from some vague desire for some impossible life, for some unwearying excitement like that of the heroine of my play." Yeats wrote the poem in 1893; the version printed in *The Bookman* in November of that year is dated October 1. In a note included with this first printing (*Variorum Edition*, p. 143) Yeats says that he has put into verse a story told him by an old woman at Ballysadare, Sligo. Ballysadare was the home of his Middleton cousins and the seat of the Pollexfen Mills. This note suggests that when Yeats came to write the poem its simple story was fully arranged in his mind. The form he chose for it is a ballad stanza of four lines, lines two and four rhyming. The fact that Yeats is retelling a story in a simple metrical form suggests that composition may have been easy, that perhaps most of the process of composing is illustrated in the versions given below. These are found on pages 20–29 and on part of page 31 of the 1893 manuscript book. The repeated reference to reeds in the first draft of the poem suggested to Yeats the title *The Wind Among the Reeds*, for on the bottom of page 19, opposite the first draft, Yeats has written, "Name for a book of verse 'The Wind among the Reeds!' "

 MacMara drove with a song
2 The wild duck and the drake
3 From the tall and tufted reeds
 Of the dim Heart Lake

 And he saw the ~~tall~~ reeds darken
6 At the coming of night tide
 And dreamed of the long brown hair
8 Of Bridget his bride

 He heard in his song and dream
10 A piper piping away
X And never was piping so mournful
11 And never was piping so sad
12 And never was piping so gay.

13 And he saw ~~that~~ young men and young girls
14 ~~Danced~~ Who danced on a level place
15 And Bridget his bride ~~danced with them~~ among them
    With a sad and a merry face

    And then they crowded about him
18 And many a sweet thing said
19 And a young man brought him red wine
    And a merry young girl white bread.

✕ But Bridget took hold of his sleeve
✕ And led him away from the throng
✕ To where old men were at cards
✕ And he went on with his song

✕ But Bridget/ his bride drew him by the sleeve
✕ Away from the dancing band
✕ To where old men were at ~~play~~ cards
✕ Twinkling their
    To old men sitting at cards
    And the twinkling of ancient hands.

    She had fear of bread and the wine
    Of those people of the air
    But he sat and played in a dream
    A dream of her long bright hair

    She had fear of the bread and the wine
    Of the people of the air
    But he sat and played in a dream
    A dream of her long dim hair

29 He played with the merry old men
✕ Nor had the thought of home
✕ Till his Bridget
    And he thought not of evil chance
31 Until one bore Bridget his bride
    Away in his arms from the dance

    And then he stood up in a rage
    And scattered the cards on the ground
✕ But the piper, the dancer and old

But the old men and young men and girls
Faded away like a cloud

X   He knew who the dancers were
X   And his heart was black with dread
     He knew who the dancers were
     And his heart was black [with] dread
     And he ran to his cabin door
     Old women that keened for the dead

41   But he heard high up in the air
42   A piper piping away
43   And never was piping so sad
44   And never was piping so gay

On the opposite page Yeats drafted what was to be his ninth stanza.

33   He bore her away in his arms
     That handsome young man there
     And his breast and his face and his arms
     Were drowned ~~by~~   in her long dark hair.

The second draft follows immediately.

 1   O'Driscoll drove with a song
 2   The wild duck and the drake
 3   From the tall and the tufted reeds
 4   Of the ~~dim~~   drear Heart Lake

     And he saw where reeds grew dark
 6   At the coming of night-tide
 7   And dreamed of the long dim hair
     Of Bridget his new wed bride.

     He heard in his song and dream
10   A piper piping away
11   And never was piping so sad
12   And never was piping so gay.

13   And he saw ~~where~~   young men and young girls
14   Who danced on a level place
15   And Bridget his bride among them
16   With a sad and a gay face

And then they/ And the dancers ~~came crowding~~   crowded about him
18 And many a sweet thing said
19 And a young man brought him red wine
   And a merry young girl white bread.

21 But Bridget drew him by the sleeve
22 Away from the merry bands
  ~~Where~~   Unto old men ~~were at~~   who played at the cards
24 With a twinkling of ancient hands;

   For the bread and the wine brought doom
26 For these were the folk of the air;
   And he played at the cards in a dream
   In a dream of her long dim hair.

29 He played with the merry old men
30 And thought not of evil chance
31 Until one bore Bridget his bride
32 Away from the merry dance.

33 He bore her away in his arms —
34 The handsomest young man there,
35 And his neck and his breast and his arms
36 Were drowned in her long dim hair

   O'Driscoll got up in a rage
38 And scattered the cards with a cry,
39 But the ~~old~~  ~~young~~  old men and ~~girls~~  dancers were gone
40 As a cloud faded into the sky

 ✕ He knew who the dancers were
 ✕ And his heart

40a He knew now the folk of the air
40b And his heart was blackened by dread
40c And he ran to ~~his cabin door~~   the door of his house
 ✕ And he [word undeciphered]
40d Old women were keening the dead;

41 But he heard high up in the air
42 A piper piping away
43 And never was piping so sad
44 And never was piping so gay.

Yeats wrote another version of stanza 10 at the bottom of page 31 of the manuscript book; it was first printed in *The Wind Among the Reeds*.

37 O'Driscoll scattered the cards
38 And out of ~~his~~ the dream awoke
39 Old men, and young men, and young girls
  Were gone like a fading smoke.

Yeats's second draft is essentially what he printed in *The Bookman*. In revising the poem for *The Wind Among the Reeds*, Yeats replaced stanza 10 with the new version given at the end of the second draft, and omitted the stanza beginning "He knew now the folk of the air." The omitted stanza tells of Bridget's death, an event already implied in her rape by the Sidhe, so the effect of the omission is to make the poem less obvious and more suggestive.

The details of Yeats's revision are less interesting than the details of his revision of "The Hosting of the Sidhe," and the revision as a whole had a far less radical effect on the poem. Even though this is true, a few of the changes Yeats made deserve particular comment: In the second draft of line 4 "dim Heart Lake" becomes "drear Heart Lake"; the word "drear" has far more emotional force than "dim," and the change has the further result of reserving "dim" for the description of Bridget's hair. Yeats revised line 5 twice: "And he saw the ~~tall~~ reeds darken" (MS. 1) / "And he saw where reeds grew dark" (MS. 2) / "And he saw how the reeds grew dark" (*Bookman*). Cutting "tall" unifies the visual impression; with it we see tall reeds in a darkening landscape, without it the darkening landscape is stressed. The revision also shifts the metrical accent from "tall" to "reeds." The revision of lines 7, 28, and 36 all involve abandoning various adjectives descriptive of hair in favor of a single adjective "dim."

 7 long brown hair (MS. 1) / long dim hair (MS. 2)
28 long bright hair / long dim hair (MS. 1)
36 long dark hair (MS. 1) / long dim hair (MS. 2)

Yeats made a change similar to those listed above in line 22 of "The Lover asks Forgiveness." The successive versions of that line go as follows: "dark shadowy hair" (MSS. 1 and 2) / "~~long~~ dim shadowy hair" (MS. 3) / "dim heavy hair" (*Wind*). In all of these revisions an adjective commonly, even tritely used to describe hair is replaced by an adjective not ordinarily used to describe hair. In the context of *The Wind Among the Reeds* I do not think this is a source of true surprise, for there the adjective "dim" seems always to hand, evocative of the Celtic twilight that pervades. In addition to contributing to this twilight effect, the changes enable Yeats to avoid certain Romantic clichés, particularly "bright hair." In revising line 9 Yeats raised a prepositional phrase to an adverbial clause: "He heard in his song and dream" (MSS. 1 and 2)/ "He heard while he sang and dreamed" (*Bookman*). Replacing nouns with verbs makes for greater energy of expression. In line 16 Yeats while revising introduced a spondaic close, a device he had used to great effect in "The Lake Isle of Innisfree." "With a sad and a merry face" (MS. 1)/ "With a sad and a gay face" (MS. 2). Finally, the changes introduced in lines 25–26 give those lines a folksy, perhaps even folk-lorish tone in keeping with the ballad meter.

> She had fear of the bread and the wine
> Of the people of the air
> (MS. 1)

> For the bread and the wine brought doom
> For these were the folk of the air
> (MS. 2)

> The bread and the wine had a doom,
> For these were the host of the air;
> (*Bookman*)

In spite of these evidences that Yeats took normal care in writing "The Host of the Air," in spite of the fact that the poem grew out of Yeats's unrequited love for Maud Gonne, it still seems all too facile. Yeats himself in "Ireland after Parnell" (1922) provides a commentary appropriate to it. There he recalls the comment of a fellow art student on one of George Russell's visionary paintings, "That is too easy, a great deal too easy!" Yeats's early poems in ballad meter strike me as a great deal too easy. They lack the verbal and technical ebullience of the late poems in ballad form, and above all they lack Yeats's marvelous, and marvelously controlling refrains. Poetry of this early sort could proliferate intolerably. Perhaps Yeats realized this, for beginning in 1895 (after he had met Diana Vernon) there came a change in his creative economy. He turned to those compact, carefully worked short lyrics that give *The Wind Among the Reeds* its characteristic autumnal tone. The poem to be studied next is a poem of this sort.

iii

## "The Lover asks Forgiveness"

ON PAGES 107–16 OF HIS MANUSCRIPT BOOK Yeats wrote out three successive drafts of "The Lover asks Forgiveness." The first of these is already highly finished; it suggests that much work had been done on the poem elsewhere. Perhaps the surest indication that Yeats thought it finished or nearly so is the carefulness with which the first of the drafts has been pointed. Yeats gave attention to pointing very late in the process of composing a poem; if a draft is carefully punctuated then it is certainly late. Each of the drafts is dated; they are the work of successive days: August 23, 24, and 25, 1895. Their special interest is that they show what Yeats could do to a poem at such close intervals. When Yeats wrote the poem he was considering an affair with Diana Vernon, and it seems to reflect his doubts and hesitations, caused by the fact that Maud Gonne pre-empted his affections. He simply could not free himself for another woman. It also reflects his belief that some apocalypse is at hand, that somehow the world from which he suffers will shortly disappear, give place to a world presided over by the Rose.

THE TWILIGHT OF ~~PEACE MY PEACE~~
FORGIVENESS

1 If this importunate heart trouble your peace
    With hopes lighter than air,
  Or plans that in mere planning flicker and cease
    Draw down your long dim hair,
  And make a twilight over your lips, and say:
    *Torn/ O piteous candle flame*
  *Wavering in winds, older than night or day,*
    *That murmuring and longing came*
  *From marble cities loud with tabors of gold,*
    *From dove-grey faery lands,*

*And/ From altars, behind purple fold on fold*
*From bridal curtains fold on purple fold*
*From bridal beds fold falling on purple fold*
            *behind many a purple fold*

12    *Queens wrought with glimmering hands;*

*From Usheen gazing on Neave's love-[pale — cancelled] lorn face*
*That saw young Neave [ride — cancelled] mourning with*
        *love-pale pale*

    *Amid the Wandering tide,*

*[From — cancelled] And lingering/ And lingered in a hidden*
        *desolate place*

16    *Where the last phoenix died,*

*And blowing the flames above his holy head;*
*[That have — cancelled] rolled the flames above his sacred head*

18    *And still murmur and long;*

*O piteous hearts that till all hearts are dead*

    *Waver in winds of song.*

Then cover the pale blossoms of your breast

    With your dark shadowy hair

And ~~bid~~   heave a sigh for ~~all~~   this heart without rest

    And/ Trouble the twilight there.
            August 22nd. 1895

## THE TWILIGHT OF FORGIVENESS

1  If this importunate heart trouble your peace

2    With words lighter than air

3  ~~Or~~   And hopes that in mere hoping flicker and cease,

    Draw down your long dim hair
    ~~Loosen~~   Unbraid your shadowy hair

And make a twilight over your lips, and say:

    *O piteous candle flame!*
    *O heart like a thin flame*

*Wavering in winds, older than night or day,*

    *That murmuring and longing came*

9 *From marble cities loud with tabors of [gold — cancelled] old,*

10    [*From* — cancelled] *In dove-grey faery lands,*
    *From* [*bridal* — cancelled] *battle curtains, fold* [*on* — cancelled]
            *upon purple fold,*

12    *Queens wrought with glimmering hands;*
    *That saw young Naeve wander with love-lorn face*
        *Amid the wandering tide*

15  *And lingered in the hidden desolate place*

16    *Where the last phoenix died*
    *And rolled the flames above his sacred head*

18    *And still murmur and long:*
    *O piteous hearts that till all hearts be dead*
        *Waver in winds of song.*

    Then cover the pale blossoms of your breast
        With your dark shadowy hair
    And heave a sigh for all hearts without rest
        And trouble the twilight there.

                ~~W B Yeats~~   August 23rd. /95

Yeats's cancellation of his own signature is charming. When Yeats signed a poem and dated it, that meant he thought the poem finished. On the next day when Yeats went to work once more, he apparently started by cancelling his signature at the end of the previous draft.

## THE TWILIGHT OF FORGIVENESS

1  If this importunate heart trouble your peace
        With ~~words~~   plans lighter than air

3  And hopes that in mere hoping flicker and cease
        Unbraid your shadowy hair

4      Crush the rose in your hair
    And shed a twilight over your lips and say:

5  Cover your lips with rose heavy twilight, and say:

6      'O hearts of windblown flame!

7  'O winds ~~older~~   elder than changing of night and day,
        'That murmuring and longing came

9 'From marble cities loud with tabors of old

10    'In dove-grey faery lands,

11 'From battle banners, fold upon purple fold

12    'Queens wrought with glimmering hands;

13 'That saw young ~~Neave~~ Niam ~~wander~~ hover with love-lorn face

14    '~~Above~~ ~~Amid~~ Above the wandering tide,

15 'And lingered in the hidden desolate place

16    'Where the last phoenix died

    'And rolled the flame above his sacred head

18    'And still murmur and long.

19 'O piteous hearts changing till change be dead

20    'In the ~~nine winds of~~ a tumultuous song'

    And cover the pale blossoms of your breast

22    With your ~~long~~ dim shadowy hair

    And bid a sigh for this heart without rest

        Trouble the twilight there.

    And trouble with sighs for all hearts longing for rest

24    The rose-heavy twilight there

                    August 24th

Yeats slightly altered lines 8, 17, 21 and 23 before printing the poem in *The Saturday Review* on November 2, 1895. We can summarize Yeats's progress by working back from the finished poem. If we ignore changes in punctuation and spelling, Yeats finished in the form first printed lines 1, 12, 16, and 18 in MS. 1; lines 2, 3, 9, 10, and 15 in MS. 2; lines 4, 5, 6, 7, 11, 13, 14, 19, 20, 22, and 24 in MS. 3. The poem reached its final form in *The Wind Among the Reeds*, except for one word; Yeats changed the archaism "elder" introduced into line 7 back to "older" in *Collected Poems*, 1933.

These drafts show how very hard Yeats was working on his diction and meter. Indeed the style of most of the poems included in *The Wind Among the Reeds* was so finished that Yeats never revised them. He achieved this finish by dint of the scrupulous care we see him exercising here. In MS. 1, for instance, Yeats uses "piteous" in line 6 and again in line 19; in MS. 2 he revises line 6 to avoid this repetition. "O piteous candle flame" becomes "O heart like a thin flame," and then in ms. 3 "O hearts of windblown flame." The successive versions of line 13 read "mourning with love-pale face"/ "wander with love-lorn face"/ "hover with love-lorn face." Here the changes seem to result from Yeats's careful adjustment of his vowel sounds. In six successive versions of line 23 Yeats at once generalizes his meaning ("this heart/ all hearts/ all things") and makes a series of delicate metrical adjustments. The number of syllables in the line shifts from 10 to 12 to 11 to 13, and the sound pattern counterpointed against the ground base of the iambic foot grows increasingly complex:

> And bid/ heave a sigh for all/ this heart without rest   (ms. 1)
> And heave a sigh for all hearts without rest   (ms. 2)
> And bid a sigh for this heart without rest   (ms. 3)
> And trouble with sighs for all hearts longing for rest   (ms. 3)
> And trouble with sighs for all hearts without rest   (sr)
> And trouble with a sigh for all things longing for rest   (*Wind*)

More interesting than these illustrations of technical care are illustrations of what might be called a depersonalizing process through which Yeats put this poem and, I think, most of the poems included in *The Wind Among the Reeds*.[1] In the first draft two lovers are together. The man asks the woman "Draw down your long dim hair/ And make a twilight over your lips, and say" — he then puts the words of the long passage in italic into her mouth. In draft 3 the intimacy of the poem has been greatly reduced, indeed even the meaning of lines 4 and 5 becomes uncertain when Yeats changes them to read "Crush the rose in your hair/ And shed a twilight over your lips and say." In revising line 11 Yeats wrote successively "bridal curtains/ bridal beds/ battle curtains/ battle banners" which again restrains the definite if vaguely expressed sexual intimacy of the first draft. A ghost of this intimacy lingers at the end of the poem when Yeats writes

> And cover the pale blossoms of your breast
>   With your dim shadowy hair
> And trouble with sighs for all hearts longing for rest
>   The rose-heavy twilight there.

Surely this poem reflects Yeats's affair with Diana Vernon, yet Yeats in his successive drafts is intentionally making this fact less apparent.

Many critics of Yeats have discussed the point at which his art had arrived when he completed *The Wind Among the Reeds*; Thomas Parkinson, Richard Ellmann, and John Unterecker seem to me to have discussed it with most insight. I have little to add to what they have already said, but since Yeats's poetry is about to take a new direction it may be useful once again to say where we are before we take off in the new direction. The situation as it appears to Yeats's present-day readers and as it seems to have appeared to him can be stated simply: Yeats never wrote more finished poetry than he wrote in *The Wind Among the Reeds*; indeed it is hard to imagine how he might have gone further along this line. Yet this poetry is far less interesting to most of his readers than his later poetry.

The explanation is partly technical. For one thing Yeats's diction has not yet achieved the metaphysical penetration which is the special characteristic of his later style:

Caught in that sensual music all neglect
Monuments of unageing intellect.

Solider Aristotle played the taws
Upon the bottom of a king of kings.

It is also instructive to observe that Yeats has not yet begun to use the various stanza forms which he perfected for his greatest poems. He does use ballad stanzas in his early poetry, though even his ballad stanzas undergo a radical development in his later poetry. Rather in *The Wind Among the Reeds* Yeats's principal effort is to write his poem in a single sentence, to make the poetic unit and the grammatic unit coincide, as John Unterecker has noted; Yeats accomplishes this surprisingly often, albeit with a little cheating by the use of frequent semicolons. He has not yet mastered a form or a diction that would be suited to a poem such as "Byzantium" or to the quite different needs of "In Memory of Major Robert Gregory."

But a more adequate explanation of the relative inadequacy of the early poems can be found if we look back to the drafts of the three poems studied above; Yeats has not yet begun to invent the forceful personae of his later poems. "The Hosting of the Sidhe" really has no persona. The theme of the poem is the theme of *The Shadowy Waters*: the attraction of an imagined, more than mortal way of life, a theme that obsessed Yeats for many years. Here it is brightly but not urgently stated. Yeats does use a persona in "The Host of the Air"; he is first called MacMara, then O'Driscoll. I don't see that it matters what he is called, since he functions in the poem very passively. And yet his situation reflects Yeats's personal situation at the time of writing; he loses his bride because of her "desire for some impossible life," for the reason Yeats feared he would lose Maud Gonne.

In the first printing of "The Lover asks Forgiveness" the poem had the title "The Twilight of Forgiveness," had, that is, no named persona. Then in *The Wind Among the Reeds* Yeats changed the title to read "Michael Robartes asks Forgiveness." Michael Robartes is one of three imagined personae — the others are Aedh and Hanrahan — into whose mouths Yeats put many of the poems included in *The Wind Among the Reeds*. Yeats's note on Michael Robartes in the original edition defined him as "fire reflected in water," as "the pride of the imagination brooding upon the greatness of its possessions, or the adoration of the Magi." All this hardly describes the voice of a man. Things became a little better in 1906 when Yeats gave the poem its present title: at least a lover is a man, not an abstraction. The trouble is that Yeats is saying what he has to say — here he is expressing his doubts and hesitations over beginning an affair with Diana Vernon while still obsessed by Maud Gonne — too tangentially, too unurgently.

Yeats has not yet solved for himself the problems of the artist's relation to his art, and to his reader. The man, W. B. Yeats, was always "involved"; at no time was he more involved than in the 1890's. But his art was not involved; it was, indeed, an antidote to rather than an expression of his own involvement. One proof of this is that none of these poems are occasional whereas most of his great poems are. One would be hard put to guess from this early poetry much of anything about the man who had contrived it, or about the political and social matrix that lay back of it. Yeats's breakthrough to a greater art, greater in all its aspects, came after he had developed the concept that poetry must be "personal utterance," though as was noted above this term needs to be carefully defined.

The earliest expression I have seen of the doctrine of "personal utterance" is found in an unpublished lecture Yeats gave in London on March 9, 1910.[2] Yeats's lecture was taken down as he spoke by an unidentified secretary; Yeats revised and corrected the manuscript produced by this secretary, part of which I quote:

One day I was at the Young Ireland Society in Dublin and took up an old newspaper, and in that old newspaper I read a ballad by some one of our obscure Irish poets. A returned emigrant was describing the first sight of the hills of his own country as he came back on shipboard. I found I was moved to tears. I said, "Why is this? It is very bad writing"; and the thought came to me, "It is because it is a man's exact feeling, his own absolute thought, put down as in a letter." I said to myself, "We have thrown away the most powerful thing in all literature — personal utterance. This poetry of abstract personality has taken the blood out of us, and I will write poetry as full of my own thought as if it were a letter to a friend, and I will write these poems in simple words, never using a phrase I could not use in prose. I will make them the absolute speech of a man."

Once the doctrine of personal utterance was worked out, Yeats's own involvements found their way into his poetry, to its great enrichment.

And yet I do not want to underrate Yeats's early verse, nor the importance of his apprenticeship. It is true that the world is largely absent from this early verse. Instead we dwell in an artistic construct, a kind of arcanum presided over by the symbolic rose. The air in this arcanum is heavy at times, the decoration sometimes over elaborate and rich. Still it is a very pleasant, not to say intoxicating place, albeit a little uncanny. Yeats took his construct very seriously; indeed, if I read "The Secret Rose" right, hoped that it would shortly displace the actual world. However this may be, Yeats worked hard at his writing then, and always. For me as for others, Yeats's revision of his early verse for *Poems*, 1895, marks the end of his apprentice years. From 1895 on his artistic means, so to speak, were adequate; he was able to express whatever he had to express, either in prose or verse, in a finished style. In a word, he was a writer, and on his way to becoming a great writer. To become one required as Yeats observed in "Reveries" that "good luck or bad luck make my life interesting." Certainly at the time Yeats thought the decade 1899–1909 a tissue of bad luck: theater business, Maud Gonne's marriage, estrangement from Ireland, the death of Synge. Yet as Thomas Parkinson has fully demonstrated in *W. B. Yeats: Self-Critic*, Yeats's experience in the theater was the crucial event in his development as a poet. Yeats could not have entered just any business: it had to be "theater business."

*2*

# Words AND
# The Wild Swans at Coole

IN the years following the publication of *The Wind Among the Reeds* Yeats wrote very few lyric poems. During the decade 1899–1909 most of his energy went into the Irish dramatic movement. With others he founded the Irish Literary Theatre in 1899, became president of the Irish National Theatre Society in 1902, and after December 27, 1904 was at times almost immersed in the affairs of the Abbey Theatre. His own writing centered in an exploration of subjects derived from Irish heroic legend in a series of plays and narrative poems. Plays exploiting Irish legend included *Cathleen ni Houlihan* (1902), *On Baile's Strand* (1903), *The King's Threshold* (1904), and *Deirdre* (1907); narrative poems such as "The Old Age of Queen Maeve" and "Baile and Aillinn" make a somewhat different use of similar materials. Yeats also wrote much prose during these years; the expanded *Celtic Twilight* appeared in 1902, *Ideas of Good and Evil* in 1903, the rewritten *Stories of Red Hanrahan* in 1904, *Discoveries* in 1907. In December 1908 Yeats began the Journal from which he later extracted "Estrangement" and "The Death of Synge."

These activities caused Yeats early in 1909 to wonder seriously if he would continue to grow as a poet. It was on February 25 that he wrote the journal entry which he slightly revised in "Estrangement XXXVIII":

43

I often wonder if my talent will ever recover from the heterogeneous labour of these last few years. The younger Hallam says that vice does not destroy genius but that the heterogeneous does. I cry out vainly for liberty and have ever less and less inner life. . . . I thought myself loving neither vice nor virtue; but virtue has come upon me and given me a nation . . . Has it left me any lyrical faculty? Whatever happens I must go on that there may be a man behind the lines already written; I cast the die long ago and must be true to the cast.

At about the same time Yeats wrote in "All Things can Tempt me"

> All things can tempt me from this craft of verse;
> One time it was a woman's face, or worse —
> The seeming needs of my fool-driven land;
> Now nothing but comes readier to hand
> Than this accustomed toil.

Yeats's talent did recover from the heterogeneous. He emerged from these activities a capable manager of theater business, a successful propagandist, and a better poet. Why Yeats's engulfment in the heterogeneous had this last effect we shall perhaps never certainly know. The ways of genius are not entirely explicable, but it is clear that bad luck had made his life interesting which meant that Yeats had more to say, and it is also clear that a decade spent in writing largely for the theater had given him wide experience in developing and handling a seemingly colloquial style. Whatever the causes, shortly after writing the laments quoted above Yeats in 1909 began once more frequently to write lyric poems, now nearly always personal utterances. The man behind the lines was a changed man with a changed conception of the nature and purpose of art. During the years 1909–19 he was to write many of his greatest poems.

*i*

## "Words"

I HAVE CHOSEN "WORDS," a simple, easily achieved poem, to show Yeats at work in 1909 because I believe that the record of its composition is fairly complete; the record includes the prose sketch or "subject," the drafts written on January 22, 1909, and the revisions of stanzas 2 and 3 made on January 23rd. Yeats wrote the poem in the Journal referred to above. The prose sketch of the poem forms section 10 of the Journal; the drafts sections 12 and 15:

Today the thought came to me that P.I.A.L. [Maud Gonne] never really understands my plans, or motives, or ideas. Then came the thought, what matter? How much of the best I have done and still do is but the attempt to explain myself to her? If she understood, I should lack a reason for writing, and one can never have too many reasons for doing what is so labourious.

  1  I had this thought an ~~hour~~  while ago
  ×  I thought of this a while
     I suddenly thought an hour ago
  2  My darling cannot understand
  3  What I have done, or what would do
  4  In this blind bitter land.
  ×  And I was dashed to think of it
     And I grew sorry thinking it
  ×  I had grown sorry at the thought
     Until my thought ~~grew clear~~  cleared up again
     Remembering that the best I have writ
     Was ~~but~~  writ to make ~~it~~  all plain.
  9  ~~How~~  That every year ~~I've~~  I have ~~said~~  cried at length
     ~~She'll~~  She can but understand it all
11  Because ~~I've~~  I have come into my strength
12  And words obey my call
  ×  ~~But~~  And had she done so — He can say
  ×  Who shook me from his sieve
  ×  If I'd have thrown poor words away
16×  And been content to live
        or else this verse
13×  ~~But~~  ~~And~~  ~~How~~  That had she done so — ~~He~~  who can say
  ×  ~~Who~~  But he that shook me from his sieve
  ×  ~~Whether~~  If I'd have thrown poor words away
16×  And been content to live.

13  That had she done so — who can say
14  What would have shaken from the sieve —
15  I might have thrown poor words away
16  And been content to live.
        January 22

The next day Yeats wrote, "The second and third stanzas of poem written yesterday should read:

   I had grown weary of the sun;
6  Until my thoughts cleared up again
7  Remembering that the best I've   have done
8  Was done to make it plain;

9   That every year I have cried 'At length
10  My darling understands it all
11  Because I have come into my strength
12  And words obey my call.' "

Comparison with the printed version shows that Yeats changed the poem very little. Once it was printed in *The Green Helmet and Other Poems*, he never revised it, though he did change the title from "The Consolation" to "Words" in *Collected Poems*, 1933. Here the process of composition was about as easy as it ever was for Yeats, perhaps because he only needed to elevate the colloquial a bit (note his careful handling of contractions) to control the very moderate heat rising from the tangential, hence self-limiting, intimacy of the poem. Colloquial language is, so to speak, one wall; arm's-length emotion is another. All Yeats had to do was to drive down the middle.

The persona is Yeats himself, the subject his own art and Maud Gonne's relation to that art. Yeats is speaking directly out of his personal situation and in his own voice. I do not see that he has much trouble here managing his I-persona. Perhaps

   That had she done so — who can say
   But he that shook me from his sieve

is slightly awkward because it interrupts the personal point of view by suggesting that God alone knows what might have happened.

   That had she done so — who can say
   What would have shaken from the sieve

is better and keeps our attention on the persona. Admittedly "Words" is a slight poem, but there has been a great increase in energy and directness of expression.

*ii*
## "The Wild Swans at Coole"

THOUGH MANUSCRIPTS OF MANY POEMS included in *Responsibil-ities* (1914) have survived, they are for the most part late drafts, and I have seen no manuscripts of some of the finest poems in the volume, such as "September 1913," and "To a Shade." *Responsibilities* is re-markable for the appearance in it of poems concerned with public issues such as the *Playboy* crisis and the controversy over Sir Hugh Lane's offer to give a collection of pictures to Dublin if a suitable gal-lery were supplied for them. Through the rest of his life Yeats contin-ued to write poems on men and events; taken together they are a splendid achievement and one almost unique in our time, since few other great poets of the twentieth century have commented so directly on our tragic history as it was being made. One could hardly deduce this history from the corpus of Wallace Stevens' poetry, and Eliot has largely confined himself to one aspect of it, the loss of traditional faith and his own efforts to regain it. Pound is occasional in his special way: he becomes occasional to denounce, with the result that he often seems to beat a dead horse. Yeats's stance is different from any of these. He addresses himself in work after work to the moral question of how modern man is to act in typical situations, in the process power-fully asserting custom and ceremony and extracting from the tradi-tions of Western man all that is most viable. The poems in which he does this are the cause, I think, of the continuing popularity of Yeats. Whereas for the special student Yeats's art may well seem to culmi-nate in such cryptic poems as "Supernatural Songs," the general reader will continue to prefer "Nineteen Hundred and Nineteen."

No complete run of drafts of any of the public-speech poems in *Responsibilities* has, so far as I know, survived. There is more material available for the study of "To a Wealthy Man" than for any other poem of its kind, but even this does not reward intensive study since it begins late in the total process of composing the poem. There are two manuscripts of the whole poem written December 24 and 25, 1912, and a corrected typescript in which the poem has reached its final form. Even the first surviving manuscript is, however, a late draft during which twenty-six of the poem's thirty-six lines were finished; most of the unfinished lines are well along toward their final wording.

The form has been set, the correlatives all assembled. Yeats has, that is, worked out his contrast of renaissance Italy and modern Dublin in all its detail.

The manuscripts of poems included in Yeats's next collection, *The Wild Swans at Coole* (1917), are likewise for the most part late drafts, and again there are not in Mrs. Yeats's collection any manuscripts at all of some of the finest poems, such as "In Memory of Major Robert Gregory"[1] and "The Double Vision of Michael Robartes." This is all the more to be regretted since beginning in 1915 and 1916, in poems such as "Ego Dominus Tuus," "The Wild Swans at Coole," and "Easter 1916," Yeats experienced a breakthrough to a greater art than he had hitherto created. Fortunately the manuscripts of "The Wild Swans at Coole" do show that poem in various stages of its creation.

Yeats's general mood, his cast of mind was reminiscent and nostalgic, though an Irish event like the revolution of 1916 could, as always, arouse his interest in an occasion. He had recently finished "Reveries over Childhood and Youth" and was continuing his autobiography in the manuscript known as "First Draft" which brings the story of his life up to 1898. It is natural that Yeats while meditating on his youth should begin his questioning of old age. This theme now moves into the very center of his poetry; in October 1916 Yeats finished "The Wild Swans at Coole," one of his greatest poems on old age. In this characteristic work Yeats uses what is nearest to him and most familiar, a walk along Coole Water, to express a universal state of mind and emotion. As he does this he achieves a diction and a rhetoric that can rightly be called noble.

Three successive drafts of the poem have survived. In all of them the order of the stanzas is as in the first printing of the poem with what is now the last stanza in the middle of the poem, following line 12. Draft A must have been written very early in the process of composition, since Yeats completed only four lines of his poem in this draft; draft B is transitional, that is it grows directly out of A and moves toward draft C; here Yeats completed thirteen lines and the whole of his original last stanza; by the end of draft C Yeats had nearly finished his poem. The three drafts are printed below.

Before he began work on draft A Yeats had established his stanza form, perhaps in still earlier drafts which have not survived. In this stanza three long lines — they range in the finished poem from eight to eleven syllables — alternate with three short lines of five, six, or

seven syllables. The basic pattern seems to my ear to place four stresses
against three with a variation of five against three at each fifth line and
occasionally elsewhere. The stanza has the unusual rhyme scheme
abcbdd. It has not occurred before in Yeats's poetry and does not exactly recur, though many years later Yeats used this rhyme scheme but
not the pattern of line lengths in "Three Songs to the Same Tune"
and the related "Three Marching Songs." The arrangement of the
rhymes varies the ababcc pattern that was a favorite scheme with
Yeats. The stanza pattern described above governs everything Yeats
does in the drafts. In this A draft the last two stanzas of the poem (in
their original order) are much less far along than the first three. The
A draft was written on two sheets of paper; there is no indication as
to their order. I have arranged the stanzas as they were first printed.
In some of the drafts of "The Wild Swans at Coole" Yeats indents his
short lines. Since this was not done consistently, I have brought all the
lines out to a uniform left margin.

### [A 1]

These/ The woods are in their autumn colours
But the Coole Water is low
× And all the paths are dry under
And all paths dry under the foot
In the soft twilight I go

The woods are in their autumn colours
× The lake narrow and bright
But the Coole Water is low
And all paths dry    The pathways hard under the footfall
× When in the twilight
× Night after night I go
Where I at twilight go
× Indolently among the trees and the stones,
× And number the wild swans.
Indolently here and there among grey stones    among the
          shadow of the grey stones
And number the wild swans.

### [A 2]

× It is now in the 19th autumn
× Since I first made my tot    count
8 Since I first made my count

&times; And now we are in the 19th year
&times; Since the first I counted

[At this point WBY marked "It is now in the 19th autumn" stet]

~~Should they~~ Should I go nearer to the
And when I go too near the water
Suddenly they'd mount
&times; And beating
Scattering, wheeling in great broken rings
On their slow clamoring wings.

25 But now they drift on the still water
&times; I have Coole's fifty nine
26 Mysterious, beautiful.
Among what waters low build nests/ rushes laid their eggs
And by what stream or pool
Where ~~will they flee~~ they have fled when I awake some day
And find they have flown away

[A 3, the verso of A 1]

They're but an image on a lake
Why should my heart [?] be wrung
&times; When I first saw them I was young
The white white unwearied [?] creatures
Delighted me when young
When I first gazed upon them

&times; Why is [it] when I gaze upon them
&times; That my heart is wrung
&times; I found it pleasing [?] to love them
&times; When I

&times; Ah now when I do gaze on them
&times; My heart, my heart is wrung
&times; And yet the white and loving/ unwearied creatures
&times; Delighted me when young

&times; And were they to clamor overhead

[A 4, the verso of A 2]

The lovely white unwearied creatures
~~Delighted~~ Always when yet young

When they flew or clamored overhead
Gave me a lighter tread

Many conquests have they
X  Their hearts have not grown cold
They have not grown old
X  By passion and by conquest
X  By lovingness and
For wander where they will
They are attended still
Passion and conquest wander where they will
24 Attend upon them still

In draft A 1 Yeats has brought together the materials of his first stanza: the trees in their autumn colors, the dry paths, the twilight, and contrasts with these emblems of old age and approaching death what seems the eternal beauty of the swans. One detail, the low water twice referred to, has been significantly changed in the finished poem where Yeats departs from the reality of the observed scene and places his swans on "brimming water." He has transferred the water, always a symbol of the sensual life in Yeats's poetry, from one set to another of the contrasting images in the stanza.

In this draft and the next Yeats introduces his I-persona, that is himself, into this stanza: "I at twilight go/ Indolently." Though beginning a poem in the first person is a frequent practice with Yeats, it would have been more frequent still had he not in instance after instance removed his I-persona from the onset of a poem late in the process of composing it. He will do this in the C drafts. Revisions of this sort are so common that we should ask what Yeats accomplished by them: many of Yeats's greatest poems begin with the setting of their symbolic scenes ("The Second Coming," the Byzantium poems, "Meditations in Time of Civil War," and "Vacillation" among others); then the persona arrives, so to speak, and when he does Yeats's meditative exploration of the scene begins. The result is that at the onset of these poems the scene itself and the themes it suggests have the reader's undivided attention. This does not happen when the persona is immediately present, for then we must divide our attention between the contemplator and what is being contemplated. Another way of putting this would be to say that the type of opening chosen involves the question whether Yeats wants the point of view to be controlling, or the view itself, or both equally. Yeats can accomplish marvels with all these strategems, but the marvels are of different sorts as one can see by comparing "The Wild Swans at Coole" with "The Tower." Shall Yeats begin as he eventually does here with youth/age, mortality/immortality, or with my age, my mortality, with the symbolic scene or with the masked man? Here too it seems to me that "indolently" introduces too much of Yeats's accidence, his state of being at the moment. When he cancels this in the B drafts we have a clear example of revision involving management of the persona.

The form of the stanza is set: even in these very early drafts Yeats never rhymes line 1 with line 3; he picks up his b rhyme at line 4 and goes on to his concluding couplet. In this draft four-stress lines alternate with three-stress lines except at line 5; in the finished poem line 3 has also five stresses. The rhyme words of the final couplet (stones, swans) are in place. Yeats has achieved very little of the diction of the finished poem: we note "autumn" and "twilight," but even that essential word "dry" has for the moment been dropped. The last line of this draft "And number the wild swans" will eventually suggest Yeats's title.

On sheet A 2 Yeats drafts his second and what was originally his third stanza. Yeats made more progress on stanza 2 than he had on stanza 1. The materials of the finished poem are all here; four rhyme words are in place (count, mount, rings, wings); line 8 is done, line 11 nearly done. Even the number of syllables in the various lines of the stanza are identical for lines 8–12 in this draft and in the finished poem: 6, 9, 5, 10, 7. The essential words are all here, though not always in their final form (scattering/ scatter, clamoring/ clamorous). Stanza 3 (now stanza 5) is as far along in its action, form and language. Here as in the finished poem the poet contemplates the drifting swans, "mysterious, beautiful," and fears that they will leave Coole Water. The line ends are in place for lines 25, 26, 28–30 (water, beautiful, pool, day, away); lines 25 and 26 are done; the pattern of line lengths is the same in the draft and the finished poem (9, 7, 8, 6, 10, 7). Most of the words found in the finished poem are here. The cancelled draft line "I have Coole's fifty-nine" will in the C drafts be effectively reworked to supply line 6.

The A 3 and A 4 drafts of the original fourth and fifth stanzas are not nearly so far along. Yeats uses all of A 3 and part of A 4 to work on his fourth stanza. Though the essential idea of the stanza, the poet's changing attitude toward the swans as he ages and they appear not to, is present, Yeats anticipates some of the material he will eventually use in his next stanza — the fact that the swans seem "unwearied," for example. No line is even near its final form. Three of the line ends are in place (creatures, head, tread), though "creatures" will be transposed to the first line of the stanza. Most of the essential words — brilliant, sore, twilight, bell-beat, trod — are still to be found. The first half of what was then Yeats's last stanza (lines 19–21) had still to be invented after these A drafts had been completed. Yeats does make good progress with the last three lines of the stanza; indeed by combining draft lines one can get

> Their hearts have not grown cold
> Passion and conquest wander where they will
> Attend upon them still.

In the A drafts Yeats has assembled most of his materials, he has established his stanza form, and found much of the diction of the finished poem. He has established eighteen line ends and completed lines 8, 25, 26, 24. He has brought stanzas 1, 2, and 3 much further toward completion than stanzas 4 and 5. In the B drafts which follow Yeats got very little further with his first three stanzas; he remade stanzas 4 and 5, indeed he completed stanza 5 in this draft. The B drafts are written on three sheets of punched paper; there are no page numbers. Yeats was undoubtedly working in a looseleaf notebook, and he seems to have followed his usual practice of writing first on the right-hand page of an opening, reserving the left-hand page for revising.

## THE SWANS AT COOLE

### [B 1]

The woods are in their autumn colours
But the lake waters are low
~~And all~~   The paths ~~dry~~   hard under the footfall
The pathways hard under the foot~~fall~~
~~And I when~~   In the pale twilight I [go]
× In the half dark I ~~will~~ go
× Indolently among the shadow of the grey stones
× And number the swans

X  Indolently among the stones and number the swans
    Among the shadow of grey stones, and number the swans
    Floating among the stones.

    We are now at the nineteenth autumn
8  Since I first made my count.
    I make no sound for if they heard me
    Suddenly they would mount
    ~~Scattering and~~  And wheel above the waters in great broken rings
    And a slow clamor of wings.

25  But now they drift on the still water
26  Mysterious beautiful
    Among what rushes will their eggs
X  Where is the stream or pool

## [B 2]

X  All will have flown to
X  All
    Upon what stream or pool
    Shall they in beauty swim, when I come here some day
    To find them flown away

X  They are but images on water
X  Why should a heart be young
    I turn away from the wat
    Why do I turn from the water;
    As though my heart were wrung
X  At how those
X  To gaze upon
    To ~~gaze~~  look upon those brilliant creatures
    I ~~did turn~~  always, when I was young
X  As they came swinging by or clamored overhead
X  I did not turn with this slow tread.
X  When they ~~when~~ swung by or
    When they came swinging by or clamored overhead
    I had a lighter tread.

[From the opposite page (verso of B 1). I have arranged the drafts in
what seems to me their proper order.]

~~I looked~~   To look upon those brilliant creatures
X  Gaily when I was young
Always when I was young
If they swung by or clamored overhead
X  I'd have a
I have trod with a lighter tread.

And yet when I was young
If they swung by, or clamored overhead
I had a lighter tread

I look upon the brilliant creatures
And am heavy and heartsore
Yet nine[teen] autumns from ~~the autumn~~ this [word undeciphered]
X  I walking upon
I hearing upon this shore
17  The bell-beat of their wings above my head
18  Trod with a lighter tread

## [B 3]

Many companions float around them
Their hearts have not grown cold
Their wings can carry them to where [they] please
Their bodies are not old
Passion and conquest dip in what stream they will
24  Attend upon them still

Companion by companion
X  And beautiful and bold
The beautiful and the bold
Have crossed the skies and climbed the river
Their hearts have not grown cold
Passion and conquest, wander where they will
24  Attend upon them still.

[From the verso of B 2]

Ah nineteen years from now
And I am growing old
They drift there lover by lover
Their hearts have not grown cold

Passion and conquest, wander where they will
24 Attend upon them still.

[The three versions of this stanza printed just above have all been cancelled.]

I turn away — lover by lover
20 They paddle in the cold
21 Companionable stream, or climb the air
22 Their hearts have not grown old
Passion and conquest, wander where they will
24 Attend upon them still.

[Yeats returned to the bottom of sheet B 2 to write two versions of line 19, the second in final form.]

X Ah lover by unwearied lover
19 Unwearied still — lover by lover

STANZA 1.   After setting an intermediate title at the top of the page, "The Swans at Coole," Yeats wrote a version of stanza 1 which develops directly from the A draft. He did not finish any of his lines, he did not even establish any additional line ends. He kept the description of the lake's low level, and his "I-persona." At line 5 in the phrase "pale twilight" he fell into a characteristic cliché of the 1890's: he tried "half-dark," but cancelled that and left his difficulty unresolved. He did drop "indolently," unfortunate because it involves us too much in his own state of mind, and reversed the order of lines 5 and 6.

STANZA 2.   Here Yeats may perhaps be said to have gone backwards. He kept his finished eighth line, and the rhyme words already established for lines 10–12; but his pattern of line lengths is no longer so nearly that found in the finished poem. He did make one important change: in this draft the swans do not rise from the surface of the lake, "I make no sound for if they heard me/ Suddenly they would mount." He then went on in his original third stanza to describe the swans floating on the lake: "But now they drift on the still water." Perhaps we have here the explanation of Yeats's transposition of stanza 3 to the end of the poem. The two contrary actions in the finished poem, the swans' flight up from the water and their floating on the water, come too close together in the poem as first printed.

STANZA 3. Yeats copied the first two lines, finished in the A drafts. He made a slight change in line 3, and then went on to invent slightly new detail for the end of the stanza when he wrote:

Upon what stream or pool
Shall they in beauty swim, when I come here some day
To find them flown away.

Again, no additional lines have been finished, no additional rhymes set.

STANZA 4. Yeats wrote four drafts of this stanza, and made great progress. At the outset he took over most of the language of the A draft; this he gradually cancelled as he achieved much of the splendid diction of the finished poem. For example, line 3 in the A draft ends with "unwearied creatures"; the swans now became "brilliant creatures" and their unweariable nature was reserved for stanza 5. Then in his fourth draft Yeats transferred "brilliant creatures" to line 1, where we find it still, and established his line ends. Here again Yeats makes a revision that involves management of his persona when he shifts from his state now at the imagined moment of the poem to his state when he first saw the swans. "I did not turn with this slow tread" involves us again in the accidence of the moment; Yeats cancels this and replaces it after several revisions by the statement that he, even nineteen years before, hearing

The bell-beat of their wings above my head
Trod with a lighter tread.

These lines are now in their final form.

STANZA 5. Yeats also made four drafts of these lines, and on his fourth try nearly finished them. These drafts provide a study in emergence. In the A drafts the swans were emblems of youth and love; they were in complete contrast with the aging man who watched them. Yeats started with these ideas, kept his b rhyme and his closing couplet, though he tried a variant of line 23 when he wrote "Passion and conquest dip in what stream they will" before re-establishing the A reading. Yeats now introduced a new idea, the fact that the swans were a company while he was alone. This led eventually to the splendid beginning of the stanza. "Many companions float around them" became

"Companion by companion"; then this was dropped down to the third line and rephrased "They drift there lover by lover." Yeats then transposed "lover by lover" to line 1:

> I turn away — lover by lover
> They paddle in the cold . . .

A false start, one more change, then the lines were done:

> ✕ Ah lover by unwearied lover
> Unwearied still — lover by lover.

While working toward his finished stanza Yeats explored and abandoned many details: should he describe the swans as "beautiful and bold"? Should he explicitly state his own age and loneliness? When the poem ended with this verse it had in some ways better balance, for we end as we will begin with the "I-persona" excluded from the first — this will happen in the C drafts — and from the final stanzas. In its original form the poem moved from the objective, to the subjective, back to the objective.

The C drafts of the poem were written on four unnumbered sheets. In this draft Yeats virtually finished his poem: twenty-two of its thirty lines are done and the others nearly done.

### [C 1]

> ✕ The woods are in their autumn foliage
> The trees are in their autumn foliage
> The water in the lake is low
> ✕ The paths of the wood are
> All pathways hard under the foot
> ✕ From stone to stone I go
> In the pale twilight I go
> Among the great grey stones I number the swans
> Floating among the stones.

[On a page which I believe was originally to the left of this, which I designate C 2, WBY redrafted this stanza in nearly final form.]

> The trees are in their autumn foliage
> 2 The woodland paths are dry
> ✕ The water ~~in~~ under the October twilight

3 Under the October twilight the water
4 Mirrors ~~the~~   a still sky
5 Upon the brimming water among ~~the stones~~   stones
6 Are nine and fifty swans

[Back to C 1]

    We are/ I am now at the nineteenth autumn
✕ From the time of my
8 Since I first made my count
    I make no sound for if they heard me
    Suddenly/ All suddenly they would mount
    Scatter and wheel in those great broken rings
    With slow clamor of their wings

25 But now they drift on the still water
26 Mysterious, beautiful
✕ Among what rushes will their eggs
✕ Upon what shore or pool
✕ Swim, when
✕ Shall five and forty dream creatures play
✕ When they have flown away
✕ Shall they disport when I awake some day
✕ To find they have fled away

[From C 2]

✕ Among what reeds
    Among what rushes do they build
28 By what lake's edge or pool
29 Delight men's eyes when I awake some day
30 To find they have flown away

    Nineteen autumns ago
    When

                    [C 3]

✕ In numbering the brilliant creatures
✕ I have numbered all the brilliant creatures
✕ And I am but heart sore

✕ I have counted five and forty two
✕ And I am more heart sore

> I turn from all those brilliant creatures
> Heavy and heart sore
> ✗ ~~And yet~~ Yet nine[teen] autumns from this evening
> ✗ I, hearing on/ upon this shore
> 17✗ The bell-beat of their wings above my head
> 18✗ Trod with a lighter tread

> 13 I have looked upon those brilliant creatures
> 14 And now my heart is sore
> 15 All's changed since I hearing at twilight
> 16 The first time on this shore
> 17 The bell-beat of their wings above my head
> 18 Trod with a lighter tread

[On the sheet opposite, that is on the verso of C 1, WBY did another version of stanza 2]

> The nineteenth autumn has gone
> Since that first time I counted
> They heard when I had but half finished
> And all suddenly mounted
> And scattered wheeling in great broken rings
> 12 Upon their clamorous wings

### [C 4]

> 19 Unwearied still — lover by lover
> 20 They paddle in the cold
> 21 Companionable streams or climb the air
> 22 Their hearts have not grown old
> Passion and conquest wander where they will
> 24 Attend upon them still

STANZA 1.   The C drafts begin with two versions of this stanza. In the first, most of the detail of the B draft recurs; in the second Yeats finished the stanza except for one word. In the first form of the stanza Yeats retained the observed detail of the low lake-water, the essential word "dry" was still missing, "pale twilight" came back, and Yeats was still very much with us as poet-protagonist. Then in the second draft the miracle occurred and the "poem comes right with a click like a closing box." To make it come right Yeats abandoned his b rhyme and wrote "The woodland paths are dry"; this had the further happy effect of taking "I go" along with it by forcing Yeats to write a new form of line 4. In place of "pale twilight" Yeats definitely established the time of the poem by writing "October twilight." He now neglected what he had observed; his imagination suggested the contrast of dry land with "brimming water" on which the swans might appropriately float. Since the "I-persona" had gone, the idea of counting the swans was dropped, and Yeats speaks instead of Coole's fifty-nine swans, a detail he had tried momentarily in draft A 2, though at another place in the poem. Yeats had still to replace "Autumn foliage" with "autumn beauty," easy to do since the line end was not involved in his rhyme scheme. The stanza is now magnificently balanced, with three autumnal images (autumn beauty, dry paths, October twilight) giving way to three images of the sensual life (water, brimming water, swans); its diction is superb.

STANZA 2.   This stanza was recalcitrant, and after the C drafts were finished Yeats had still more work to do on it than on any other part of the poem. In the draft on C 1, which takes off directly from the B drafts, Yeats retains the idea of not disturbing the swans as they float on Coole Water. He made slight verbal rearrangements as when "And wheel above the waters in great broken rings" became "Scatter and wheel in those great broken rings." Then on the verso of C 1 Yeats tried another version. He dropped the idea of not disturbing the swans. Now instead of merely imagining what would happen if they were disturbed, he recalls their flight from the lake nineteen years before. For the moment he has phrased the stanza in the past tense: "heard," "mounted," "scattered." His principal revision changes these verbs to the present tense. Only line 12 is done, but lines 10 and 11 are nearly done. Line 8, the first line of the poem to be finished, has for the moment been changed.

STANZA 3.   Here, as with stanza 1, Yeats made great progress. He began by copying out his finished opening lines (25, 26), then went on to explore detail that might fill out his stanza. The progressive versions of line 29 illustrate this exploration:

Shall five and forty dream creatures play
Shall they disport when I awake some day
Delight men's eyes when I awake some day.

With the invention of the line just quoted, the stanza suddenly came right; all the lines save line 27 are done; that nearly done.

STANZA 4.   Yeats began by slightly changing the action that takes place in this stanza in the B drafts, where Yeats looked at the swans. He now explored the idea of counting them again, then turning away from them, before he returned to a slight revision of B, "I have looked upon those brilliant creatures." When Yeats abandoned his second explicit reference to his condition now compared with his condition nineteen years before, the stanza came right. He has stated again the essential theme of the poem, the contrast of youth and age, but in more general terms:

> All's changed since I hearing at twilight
> The first time on this shore.

Yeats concluded the stanza with his already finished seventeenth and eighteenth lines.

STANZA 5.   This has the same form as in the B drafts.

During the course of these three drafts Yeats completed lines 2–6, 8, 12–22, 24–26, 28–30, and his unfinished lines required only slight correction before reaching the form in which they were first printed. The final word in line 1 was changed from "foliage" to "beauty"; in line 23 "and" became "or"; the verb in line 27 was changed from "do" to "will." Stanza 2 was rewritten before it was printed. I place the manuscript version above the version printed:

> The nineteenth autumn has gone
> Since that first time I counted
> They heard when I had but half finished
> And all suddenly mounted
> And scattered wheeling in great broken rings
> Upon their clamorous wings

> The nineteenth autumn has come upon me
> Since I first made my count;
> I saw, before I had well finished,
> All suddenly mount
> And scatter wheeling in great broken rings
> Upon their clamorous wings.

Once printed, the text of "The Wild Swans at Coole" remained unchanged except for Yeats's decision to place what was originally his final stanza in the middle of his poem. This change first appeared in the Cuala Press edition of *Wild Swans*. We have already speculated about Yeats's reasons for making this change.

The doctrine of personal utterance is clearly operative both in "Words" and in "The Wild Swans at Coole," though the great difference in dimension and quality of the poems already suggests that a personal utterance should not be too personal. In both poems Yeats is writing of his own life, but perhaps only in the second has he made of it "something intended, complete," achieved that is the ideal stated in 1937 in "The First Principle." This achievement accounts for the increasing power of his verse. The breakthrough to controlled personal utterance came with "Adam's Curse" (written 1902, see *Letters*, p. 382) and affects all the poems printed with *The Green Helmet*, poems written in the years 1908–11, among them "Words." These are not Yeats's greatest poems, though "No Second Troy," "The Fascination of What's Difficult," and "Brown Penny" are fine poems, but with them we have clearly left behind the hermetic world of *The Wind Among the Reeds*. We hear of land agitation and the Abbey Theatre, we discover in "At Galway Races" the onset of lines of speculation that will engross Yeats for many years — the ideal relation of the poet and the man of action (the horseman) which will come with the dawn of a new age.

In *Responsibilities* a breakthrough to a larger audience is achieved when in "To a Wealthy Man" and "September 1913" Yeats writes the first of his great "public speech" poems. In *The Wild Swans at Coole* Yeats's mood seems meditative — seems because Yeats reserved for his next volume the poems inspired by the Easter Rebellion, all splendid examples of public speech and all written before the content of *Swans* was set in the volume Macmillan published in 1919. "The Wild Swans at Coole" is a typical and brilliant Yeatsean meditation, clearly a personal utterance from first to last which already avoids the danger that mere accidence may intrude into and spoil such an utterance. It illustrates the enlargement of Yeats's art which took place during these middle years, an enlargement that is intellectual as well as technical. A personal utterance becomes public speech in "Easter 1916" (as yet only privately printed); this mode of poetry was more and more to prevail.

# Nineteen Hundred and Nineteen

THE years 1918–20 were particularly fruitful for Yeats. His personal life had settled into a satisfactory pattern at last. He was intellectually and emotionally stimulated by those strange experiences described in "A Packet for Ezra Pound." His playwriting, now that he had adapted the Noh form to his dramatic purposes, was going so well that in 1919 he was at last delivered from that succubus, *The Player Queen*. But his euphoria is most apparent in his poetry, which reaches now one of its greatest moments in poems such as "The Second Coming," "A Prayer for my Daughter," "All Souls' Night," and "Nineteen Hundred and Nineteen." Jon Stallworthy has printed and analysed the manuscripts of "The Second Coming" and "A Prayer for my Daughter" in *Between the Lines*. I have chosen "Nineteen Hundred and Nineteen" for study, even though the surviving drafts begin at a late point in the total process of the poem's creation, chosen it because of the greatness of the poem and because these surviving drafts do constitute a typical manuscript. These drafts include three manuscripts and a typescript which I have designated MS. 1, MS. 2, TS. 1, and MS. 3. MS. 1 was written on ten unnumbered sheets of unlined notebook paper; MS. 2 is a clean copy of MS. 1 written on seven sheets of the same paper, numbered by Yeats; TS. 1 is a transcript of MS. 2 on five sheets of standard typing bond, numbered and stapled; MS. 3 (containing further drafts of lines 9–32 only) is written on five sheets, four of letter and one of notebook paper, unnumbered, and without other external evidence of the order of drafts. I am responsible for the order in which MS. 1 and MS. 3 are printed.

Even in MS. 1 Yeats has already assembled most of his concourse of emblems and correlatives; he has worked out the intricate stanza patterns used in the various parts of the poem, with all their delicate shifts in line lengths, and stress and rhyme patterns; he has found most of the diction of the finished poem; the manuscript is carefully punctuated. It is undoubtedly a late draft, as the following table will further establish.

> Part I.   29 lines are done as in the first printing; 14 lines have rhyme words established or virtually established; 5 lines have rhyme sounds established or virtually established. This accounts for all 48 lines.
>
> Part II.   Finished
>
> Part III.   All lines are finished save 69 and 79, and these require only the change of a single word.
>
> Part IV.   Finished
>
> Part V.   All lines are finished save 93, 103, and 107; these require only minor adjustments.
>
> Part VI.   Finished, save for a tense shift (weary/ wearied) in line 116.
>
> NOTE.   The substance and much of the language of the explanatory note to Part VI is found in the manuscript.

This table shows that only part I of the poem required much additional work.

From the drafts described above I print the whole of MS. 1, interesting even when it reaches final form because of the many verbal changes made; part I from MS. 2; and the whole of MS. 3.

[MS. 1, page 1]

THE THINGS ~~RETURN~~ ~~COME~~ THAT COME AGAIN

I

1  Many ingenious lovely things are gone
2  That seemed sheer miracle to the multitude;
Changeless and deathless; above the murdering moon
Above the insolence of the sun. There stood
Where many a gold and silver paten shone
6  An ancient image made of olive wood;

7  And gone are Phidias' carven ivories
8  And all his golden grasshoppers and bees.

9   We too had many pretty toys when young:
10  A law indifferent to blame or praise,
    A speedy remedy for obvious wrong
    No swaggering soldier on the public ways
    Who weighed a man's life lighter than a song;
    A general confidence in future days
    In some great thing to come, because we thought
16  That the worst rogues and rascals had died out.

[Page 2]

    And we would say if conversation turned
    On ignorance and armies and such things
    That all men soon would be both fed and learned;
    That armies now that parliaments and kings
    No more might covet what they had not earned
    Existed for their drums and fiddle strings
    And did the cannon sound 'twere but perchance
    To make a guardsman's lazy charger prance

X  But our good dream is spent, once
X  That good dream has had its day
    But now in place of comfortable dreams nightmare
    ~~Returns again~~   Can ride again, a drunken soldiery
27  ~~May~~   Can leave the mother murdered at her door
28  To crawl in her own blood and go scot free;
X  Night shakes with terror as it shook before
29  The night can sweat with terror as before
30  We pieced our thoughts into philosophy
31  And planned to bring the world under a rule
32  Who are but weasels fighting in a hole.

X  Henceforth let no man
X  Who dare now fancy that his work will stand
X  Whether ambition wrought or pure intent
X  And whether work of mind or work of hand;
X  And that he may keep pride of intellect
X  Nor by vain hope nor by despair unmanned

✕ I'd give him one dear thought: all triumph would
40✕ But break upon his ghostly solitude

[Page 3]

33 He ~~would~~   who can read the signs, nor sink unmanned
34 Into the half deceit of some intoxicant
35 From shallow ~~brains~~   wits; who knows no work can stand
36 Whether health, wealth, or peace of mind were spent
✕ On work of ~~mind~~   intellect, or work of hand
✕ No passion leave a lasting monument
✕ Has but one comfort left: all passion would
40✕ But break upon his ghostly solitude.

37 On masterwork of intellect or hand
38 No ~~passion~~   honour leave ~~eternal~~   its mighty monument
39 Has but one comfort left — all triumph would
40 But break upon his ghostly solitude

[Page 4]

✕ For all the rest is but love's bitterest wound:
41 And other comfort were a bitter wound
✕ Hope set upon what fades and vanishes;
42 To be in love and love what vanishes;
43 Greeks were but lovers, all that country round
   Who dared admit, if such a thought were his,
45 Incendiary or bigot could be found
46 To burn that stump on the Acropolis
47 Or break in bits the famous ivories,
48 Or traffic in the grasshoppers and bees.

[Page 5]

   II

✕ When Loie Fuller's chinese dancers ~~enwound~~   unwound
✕ Suddenly that long ribbon of shining cloth
50✕ ~~Suddenly~~   A shining web, a floating ribbon of cloth
✕ It seemed a dragon of the air
✕ Had fallen upon them and turned them round and round
✕ Fallen upon their paths had turned them round
✕ Or caught them up on its own whirling path
✕ Or carried them off ~~on its~~   to its own whirling path

54✕ ~~The great~~   So the Platonic year
55✕ Whirls out new right and wrong
56✕ Whirls in the old instead
57✕ All men are dancers ~~and tread~~   and their tread
58✕ Goes to the barbarous clangour of a gong

II

49 When Loie Fuller's Chinese dancers enwound
50 A shining web, a floating ribbon of cloth
✕ It seemed a dragon of air
✕ Suddenly fallen had whirled them around
51 It seemed that a dragon [of] air
✕ Suddenly fallen had whirled them round and round
✕ Had fallen of a sudden and whirled them around
✕ ~~Had fallen~~   Suddenly fallen among dancers, whirled them round
52 Had fallen among dancers, had whirled them round
✕ Or swept them away to its own furious path
53 Or hurried them off on its own furious path;
54 So the Platonic Year
55 Whirls out new right and wrong
56 Whirls in the old instead
57 All men are dancers and their tread
58 Goes to the barbarous clangour of a gong.

[Page 6]

III

59 Some moralist or mythological poet
60 Compares the solitary soul to a swan;
61 I am content with that,
62 Contented that a troubled mirror show it
63 Before that brief gleam of its life be gone
64 An image of its state;
65 The wings half spread for flight
66 The breast thrust out in pride
67 Whether to play or to ride
68 Those winds that clamour of approaching night.

A man in his most secret meditation
70 Is lost amid the labyrinth that he has made

71  In art or politics,
72  Some Platonist affirms that in the station
73  Where we should cast off body and trade
74  The ancient habit sticks
75  And that if our works could
76  But vanish with our breath
77  That were a lucky death
78  For triumph can but mar our solitude

    The swan has leaped into a desolate heaven;
80  That ~~thought brings~~  image can bring wildness, bring a rage
81  To end all things, to end
82  What my laborious life imagined, even
83  The half imagined, the half written page;

[Page 7]

84  O but we dreamed to mend
85  Whatever mischief seemed
86  To afflict mankind but now
87  That winds of winter blow
88  Learn that we were crack-pated when we dreamed.

    I V

89  We who seven years ago
90  Talked of honour and of truth
91  Shriek with pleasure if we show
×   Weasel
92  The weasel's twist, the weasel's tooth.

[Page 8]

    v

    Come let us mock the great
94  That had such burdens on the mind
95  And toiled so hard and late
96  To leave ~~some~~   ~~that~~   some monument behind
97  Nor thought of the leveling wind.

98  Come let us mock at the wise;
    ~~With~~   For all those calendars, whereon
100  They fixed old aching eyes,

101 They never saw how seasons run
102 And now but gape at the sun

    And after mock at the good
  ✕  That thought even goodness might be gay
  ✕  Who thought mere goodness might be gay
104 That fancied goodness might be gay
105 Grown tired of their solitude,
106 Upon some bran-new happy day:
    Wind shrieks and where are they:

108 Mock ~~poets~~ mockers after that
109 That would not lift a hand maybe
110 To help good, wise, or great
  ✕  To shut the ~~north~~ bleak winds out for ~~we~~ ~~he~~ we
  ✕  Delight in mockery
  ✕  Are heartened by mockery
  ✕  Delight in mockery
  ✕  Love bitter mockery
  ✕  To ~~shut the foul storm out~~ shutter out the storm for we
  ✕  Traffic in mockery
111 To bar ~~that tempest~~ that foul storm out, for we
112 Traffic in mockery.

## [Page 9]

### VI

113 Violence upon the roads: violence of horses
114 Some few have handsome riders, are garlanded
115 On delicate sensitive ear or tossing mane
    But weary running round and round in their courses
117 ~~They~~ All break and vanish and evil gathers head:
118 Herodias' daughters have returned again
119 A sudden blast of dusty wind and after
120 Thunder of feet, tumult of images
121 Their purpose in the labyrinth of the wind
122 And should some crazy hand dare touch a daughter
123 All turn with amorous cries, or angry cries
124 According to the wind for all are blind.
  ✕  But with the ~~settled~~ settling dust worse company
125 But now wind drops, dust settles; thereupon

$\times$ There lurches there his great eyes without thought
126 There lurches past his great eyes without thought
127 Under the shadow of stupid straw-pale locks
$\times$ Infamous Robert Artisson of Kilkenny
$\times$ There lurches by that infamous Robert Artisson
128 That insolent fiend Robert Artisson
129 To whom the love-lorn Lady Kyteler brought
130 Bronzed peacock feathers, red combs of her cocks

> Note: The country people see at times certain apparitions whom they name now "fallen angels," now "the ancient inhabitants of the country," and describe as riding "with flowers upon the heads of their horses." I have assumed in the sixth poem that these comely apparitions, now that the times worsen, give way to worse. Robert Artisson was an evil spirit much run after in Kilkenny at the start of the fourteenth century. Are not those who travel in the whirling dust also in the Platonic Year?
>
> WBY.

*Further notes on* MS. 1:

*Part* I.   Lines 3–5 were altered after MS. 2 was written, and before the poem was first printed. They reached final form in *The Tower*, 1928. Lines 9–26 were completed in MS. 3, printed below. Lines 41–43 have the form in which they were first printed; they also reached final form in *The Tower*, 1928. The remaining lines (1–2, 6–10, 16, 27–43, 45–48) have reached their final form.

*Part* II.   The changes made in this draft improve Yeats's diction and phrasing. The pattern of the elaborate stanza must have been set in earlier drafts, and all the materials assembled.

*Part* III.   Lines 61–62 reached final form in *The Tower*, 1928. In line 69 "most secret" became "own secret" and in line 79 "into a desolate" became "into the desolate" in MS. 2.

*Part* V.   Yeats completed lines 93 and 103 when he decided to repeat three times the clause "Come let us mock at the." He finished line 93 in MS. 2, line 103 after MS. 2. In line 107 a shift of tense (shrieks/ shrieked) occurs in MS. 2. The change from "Mock poets" to "Mock mockers" at line 108 particularly interests me. I suspect Yeats made it for doctrinal reasons. While Yeats thought that the man who was also an artist should be engaged, he thought that the artist *per se* should have no faith except a faith in works. He had quoted Balzac to that effect many years before in an essay dropped from *Discoveries*. The successive versions of lines 111 and 112 show two fine lines emerging from a series of characteristic changes in wording. Lines 105–6 reached final form in *The Tower*, 1928.

As was noted above, MS. 2 is little more than a clean copy of MS. 1. Yeats did finish one additional line of part 1 (44). I print part 1 from this MS. so that the record of its composition may be as complete as possible.

[MS. 2, part 1, page 1]

## THOUGHTS UPON THE PRESENT STATE OF THE WORLD

I

1 Many ingenious lovely things are gone
2 That seemed sheer miracle to the multitude,
Changeless, deathless, above the murdering moon,
Above the insolence of the sun. There stood
Where many a gold and silver paten shone
6 An ancient image made of olive wood;
7 And gone are Phidias' carven ivories
8 And all his golden grasshoppers and bees.

9 We too had many pretty toys when young:
10 A law indifferent to blame or praise;
A speedy remedy for obvious wrong;
No swaggering soldier on the public ways
Who weighed a man's life lighter than a song;
A general confidence in future days,
In some great thing to come, because we thought
16 That the worst rogues and rascals had died out.

[Page 2]

And we would say, if conversation turned
On ignorance and armies and such things,
That all men soon would be both fed and learned;

That armies, now that parliaments and kings
No more might covet what they had not earned,
Existed for their drums and fiddle strings,
And did the cannon sound 'twere but perchance
To make a guardsman's lazy charger prance.

&times; But that good dream has had its day; nightmare
&times; Comfortable dreams are gone; nightmare
~~Can ride again~~ In place of comfortable dreams night-mare
Can ride our sleep; a drunken soldiery
27 ~~May~~ Can leave the mother, murdered at [her] door,
28 To crawl in her own blood and go scot free;
&times; Night shakes with terror as it shook before
&times; Night sweats with terror as those nights before
&times; And the night sweats with terror as before
29 The night can sweat with terror as before
30 We pieced our thoughts into philosophy
31 And planned to bring the world under a rule
32 Who are but weasels fighting in a hole.

&times; Who now dare fancy that his work will stand
&times; Whether ambition wrought or pure intent
&times; His passion find a lasting monument
&times; ~~And~~ Whether on work of mind or work of hand
&times; And that he may keep pride of intellect
&times; Health wealth or peace of mind were spent
&times; Nor mocked by hope nor by despair unmanned

### [Page 3]

&times; This certainty remains: all triumph would
40&times; But break upon his ghostly solitude
&times; For all the rest is but love's bitterest wound:
&times; Hope set upon what fades and vanishes.
43&times; Greeks were but lovers; all that country round
&times; Who dared admit, if such a thought were his,

&times; Who now dare fancy that his work will stand?
&times; Whether health, wealth, or peace of mind were spent
&times; Upon some work of intellect or hand,
&times; Who thinks to leave a lasting monument
&times; Makes nothing but the devil's rope of sand;

✕ Let storm turn up the sand and be content
✕ With one dear thought of thoughts: all triumph would
✕ But break upon our ghostly solitude

✕ Makes but a devil's rope out of the sand
✕ For wind must gather what the wind has sent
✕ And may be that is well

33 He who can read the signs, nor sink unmanned
34 Into the half deceit of some intoxicant
35 From shallow wits, who knows no work can stand,
36 Whether health, wealth, or peace of mind were spent
37 On master work of intellect or hand,
38 No honour leave its mighty monument,
39 Has but one comfort left: all triumph would
40 But break upon his ghostly solitude.

[Page 4]

✕ For all the rest is but love's bitterest wound:
41 And other comfort were a bitter wound:
✕ Hope set upon what fades and vanishes;
42 To be in love and love what vanishes;
43 Greeks were but lovers, all that country round
44 ~~Who~~ None dared admit, if such a thought were his,
45 Incendiary, or bigot, could be found
46 To burn that stump on the Acropolis,
47 Or break in bits the famous ivories,
48 Or traffic in the grasshoppers and bees?

Stanzas 1, 2, and 3 (lines 1–24) are verbally identical in MS. 1 and MS. 2. MS. 2 is more carefully punctuated. Beginning with stanza 4, MS. 2 ceased to be merely a clean copy, for Yeats began to cancel lines and make verbal changes. He did little more, however, than explore the possibilities inherent in MS. 1. On pages 2 and 3 of the manuscript, he wrote and cancelled a series of versions of stanza 5 and the first half of stanza 6, but at the bottom of page 3 he reinstated verbatim the version of stanza 5 he had written in MS. 1. In the draft of stanza 5 found in the middle of page 3 Yeats explored two new details which might possibly serve as emblems of the transientness of works of art and intellect: the devil's rope of sand, and, in "For wind must gather what the wind has sent," possibly the Sibylline leaves. He abandoned both. In MS. 1 stanza 6 had been completed except for line 44. Yeats tried a slightly different wording of the first half of this stanza on page 3 of the manuscript, but cancelled this. On page 4 he reinstated the readings of MS. 1, but did finish line 44.

Save for lines 3–5 and 11–26 Yeats now had part 1 of his poem in the form he first printed it. I have seen no manuscript of Yeats's revision of lines 3–5, which were changed before first printing and again in *The Tower*, 1928. Below is MS. 3, a series of versions of lines 11–26. In the last of them these lines have their final form.

[MS. 3, page 1]

X And if we still had empire and such things

> We dreamed, though we had empire and such things
> Their teeth were drawn, their ancient tricks unlearned
> What matter if no parliaments nor kings
> Had made their guns be all to ploughshares turned
> Women love shows. Mere drum and fiddle string
> Unless some tons of gunpowder were burned
> Had not made uproar great enough perhaps
> To make some guardsman's drowsy charger prance.

9 We too had many pretty toys when young:
10 A law indifferent to blame or praise
  To bribe or threat; all obvious wrong
X Melted like sun warmed wax
X Melted as it were wax in the sun's rays
  Half melted down like wax in the sun's rays:
X A public conscience
13 Public opinion, ripening for so long
  We thought it would outlast all future days:
15 O what fine thoughts we had because we thought
16 That the worst rogues and rascals had died out

[Page 2]

9 We too had many pretty toys when young:
10 A law indifferent to blame or praise,
  To bribe or threat; all obvious wrong
  Half melted down like wax in the sun's rays;
13 Public opinion ripening for so long
14 We thought it would outlive all future days;

15 ~~And~~   O what fine thoughts we had because we thought
16 That the worst rogues and rascals had died out.

We dreamed, though we had empires and such things,
Their teeth were drawn, their ancient tricks unlearned;
What matter if no parliaments nor kings
Had made their guns be all to ploughshares turned;
X Women love shows; mere drums and fiddle strings
X Women love shows — ~~yet~~   but drums and fiddle strings
X Women love shows; ~~yet drums and~~   how could mere trumpetings,
X Unless some tons of gunpowder were burned,
X Might not make uproar great enough ~~perhaps~~   perchance
X To make some guardsman's drowsy charger prance.

25 X Now days are dragon ridden, the nightmare
X Riding our sleep: a drunken soldiery

Women love horses; though an army brings
Trumpet and kettle but no powder burned
The uproar is not great enough perchance
To make a guardsman's drowsy charger prance.
25 Now days are dragon ridden, the nightmare
Riding our sleep

## [Page 3]

9 We too had many pretty toys when young:
10 A law indifferent to ~~praise or to~~   blame, or praise,
To bribe or threat; all obvious wrong
Half melted down like wax in the sun's rays;
13 Public opinion ~~ripened~~   ripening for so long
14 We thought it would outlive all future days;
15 O what fine thoughts we had because we thought
16 That the worst rogues and rascals had died out.

We dreamed, though we had empire and such things,
Their teeth were drawn, their ancient tricks unlearned;
What matter if no parliaments nor kings
Had made their guns be all to ploughshares turned;
X Women love shows
An army is for show and though it brings

Trumpet and kettle if no powder's burned
The uproar is not great enough, perchance,
To make a guardsman's drowsy charger prance.

25 Now days are dragon ridden, the nightmare
   Is riding sleep: a drunken soldiery

### [Page 4]

17 All teeth ~~are~~   were drawn, all ancient tricks unlearned
18 And a great army but a showy thing;
19 What matter that no cannon ~~has~~   had been turned
20 Into a ploughshare; parliament and king
21 ~~Think~~   Thought that unless a little powder burned
22 The trumpeters ~~may~~   might burst with trumpeting
23 And yet it lack all glory, and perchance
24 The guardsmen's drowsy chargers ~~will~~   would not prance

25 Now days are dragon ridden, the nightmare
 ✕  Is riding
   Riding upon sleep

### [Page 5]

 9 We too had many pretty toys when young:
10 A law indifferent to blame or praise
11 To bribe or threat; habits that made old wrong
 ✕ Dissolve away like wax
12 Melt down, as it were wax in the sun's rays;
13 Public opinion ripening for so long
   We thought it would outlast all future days.
15 O what fine thought we had because we thought
16 That the worst rogues and rascals had died out.

17 All teeth were drawn, all ancient tricks unlearned,
18 And a great army but a showy thing;
19 What matter that no cannon had been turned
20 Into a ploughshare; parliament and king
21 Thought that unless a little powder burned
22 The trumpeters might burst with trumpeting
23 And yet it lack all glory; and perchance
24 The guardsmen's drowsy chargers would not prance.

25 Now days are dragon ridden, the nightmare
26 ~~Riding~~   Rides upon sleep: a drunken soldiery

On page 1 of MS. 3 Yeats began with a radical attack on stanza 3 (lines 17–24). He tried reversing the a and b rhymes used in MSS. 1 and 2 (the rhyme pattern of the stanza is abababcc), and explored possible new detail that could express man's social hope before World War I. Much of this he kept in his finished poem. His new detail included a reference to empire; the drawn teeth, the ancient tricks unlearned, and the swords beaten into ploughshares found in the finished poem; the notion that because women love shows powder must be burned so horses will prance. He has accumulated too many correlatives; in later drafts he dropped the reference to empire and to the women who love shows, though he did not drop this last detail until after it had caused him a great deal of trouble. Yeats didn't finish any of his lines, but he did make a new beginning. The draft of stanza 2 (lines 9–16) on the bottom of the same manuscript page was also a crucial draft. Lines 12 and 13 in MS. 2 read

> No swaggering soldier on the public ways
> Who weighed a man's life lighter than a song.

This is a specific reference to the Black-and-Tans and would have been recognized as such by Irish readers, a reference, that is, to the violence going on in the world as Yeats wrote his poem. But his subject in this stanza and the one that follows is the nonviolent civilization that had existed before 1914. Yeats replaced this anticipation of his thought in stanza 4 by the simile of wrong melting like wax, and went on to his reference to ripening public opinion. These changes cleared up the logical progression of the poem, and they enabled Yeats to finish lines 13 and 15, nearly to finish line 14.

Yeats began page 2 of these drafts by making a clean copy of the lines he had just written; while doing this he finished line 14 when he replaced "it would outlast" by "it would outlive." (He reinstated the earlier reading on page 5 of this MS.) He then did another version of lines 17–26, in which the a and b rhymes are still reversed. Most of his difficulties here grew out of his efforts to give poetic substance to the idea that because "women love shows" some powder had to be burned in order to make the chargers prance. While trying and cancelling line after line, Yeats did invent "trumpetings" to replace the "drum and fiddle strings" of earlier drafts. He went on to finish line 25 by introducing into it the phrase "dragon ridden," a preparation for the "dragon of air" in part II, which was already finished. This preparation for a coming central image is as characteristic of Yeats as it is of Proust. Though he cancelled the line after first writing it, he reinstated it at the bottom of the page. Just above this he tried another, more logical version of lines 21–24: now "women love horses," and it is the burning powder that makes the horses prance.

Page 3 begins with a further version of stanza 2, identical with that on the top of page 2. The rhymes are still reversed in the draft of stanza 3 which follows, but Yeats did give up here the attempt to make anything of the "women love shows" business. When he cancelled this and wrote "An army is for show" he has expressed the central idea of stanza 3 in the finished poem. On page 4 a characteristic miracle of organization occurs, and Yeats finishes stanza 3. He puts his a and b rhyme words back into the order they had had in MSS. 1 and 2. The crucial event occurred, I think, when Yeats established line 18

And a great army but a showy thing;

the stanza took shape around this line. Every detail, nearly every word or phrase used has occurred somewhere or other during the course of many drafts, but Yeats till now had failed to fuse them together in their inevitable order. The clause "And yet it lack all glory" is likewise a new invention. It is instructive to note that both are general statements around which what had been a clutter of detail can logically accumulate. At the bottom of the page Yeats nearly finishes line 26.

On page 5 Yeats finished his second stanza. Here the crystallizing took place when Yeats invented the clause "habits that made old wrong/ Melt down." He went on to make a clean copy of stanza 3. At the very bottom of the page he got line 26 right when he changed to the present tense in "the nightmare/ Rides." This urgently states the contrast of past with present. Lines 19–26 were done at last, and one of Yeats's greatest poems, "Nineteen Hundred and Nineteen," done but for a little subsequent touching up.

We noticed that Yeats's difficulties here clustered around the phrase "women love shows," and that the offending lines did not come right until Yeats dropped this detail entirely. Again we have revision involving management of the persona. The persona of "Nineteen Hundred and Nineteen" is Yeats himself in the role of vatic poet commenting on events, though Yeats in the finished poem reserved the first person till section III where he shifts to direct commentary. The "women love shows" idea is destructive of this persona. How can it coexist with the mother murdered? Yeats's final idea that an army is a showy thing is appropriate to the voice that laments and speaks the poem. Here Yeats revises to build his persona.

*4*

# The Tower, Section III,
# AND Lullaby

*i*

## "The Tower," Section III

THE SUCCESSIVE DRAFTS of some of the great poems Yeats wrote during the 1920's have survived; we are now able, perhaps for the first time with the poems studied in this book, to follow Yeats through the entire process of composing a poem. I have chosen part of section III of "The Tower" to illustrate this process because of the state in which the rough drafts have been preserved. Yeats composed them in a loose-leaf manuscript cover. Occasionally, as in this instance, looseleaf workbooks have been preserved with drafts of various items of prose and verse still in them. Usually when Yeats had dictated from such drafts or had them transcribed, he withdrew the sheets and filed them in an envelope. A probable explanation of the few manuscript covers with drafts still in them is that Yeats had been given a new cover — manuscript covers and manuscript books were gifts he much appreciated — and abandoned the old one just as it stood.

Whatever the explanation, we can be fairly certain that the pages containing the early versions of section III of "The Tower" are preserved just as Yeats left them. Sometime after writing these early drafts of "The Tower," Yeats completed a manuscript of the entire poem on October 7, 1925. A typescript with two carbons was made of this manuscript, and Yeats made corrections on all three copies. Type-script 2, which has no manuscript revisions, was made from these corrected copies of TS. 1. In it the poem nearly reached the form in which it was first printed.

When writing in a manuscript book or looseleaf cover, Yeats nor-mally started to work on the right-hand page and used the facing page for revisions. So in the transcription printed below, I first give these right-hand pages; then, below each of them, the facing page. When the facing page is blank, no "facing page" is given.

[Page 1]

× It is time give [?] I my testament
   [Undeciphered line]

× O
× Old men
× An old man makes his testament
× And I
× And this is mine

× Now will I write my testament
× And choose
× And choose once more for an heir
× Young men

   I write my testament being old
× And choose for an heir young men and tall
× And chose once, that tall young man
× Some tall young man shall be my heir
× Climbed a mountain stream in the cold
× Many dawns
× Climbing a mountain stream in the cold
   ~~Casts a fly~~   Drops a fly ~~under~~   in the cold
× Dawn light upon the bare

[Facing page 1]

   And choose a sunflecked man for an heir
× That can climb up a cold mountain
   ~~I choose a tall young~~   man for an heir
   ~~A man that fishes~~   That clambers up a cold
   Mountain stream on Ochte's bare [1]

Or Bulben's woody side, and at dawn ~~throws~~
&times; Throws a
&times; A fly under a fly under a froth
Throws a deft fly ~~among the froth~~   under the side
&times; Under a dark stone
&times; Under the edge of a dark stone
Of a great ~~foam~~   froth.

[Page 2]

&times; Morning
&times; Dawn light,
Mountain stream on Ochte's bare
&times; And
Or Bulben

I write my testament being old
I choose a stalwart man for my heir
&times; And
&times; Through him climbing a [?]
And summon him from a cold
Mountain stream upon Ochte's bare
Or Bulben's shaded side where at dawn
&times; He has dropped a fly
&times; He cast amid the eddying froth
&times; Even that
&times; He cast for
His trout fly dropped amid the froth
A young imaginative man
In rough grey Connemara cloth

[Facing page 2]
I choose ~~out~~   young outstanding men
&times; ~~Men~~   That climb up ~~the~~   little
&times; That climb up the rocks

[Page 3]
145 And I declare my faith
146 I mock Plotinus' thought
    ~~Declare~~   Aye, and in Plato's teeth
    ~~I cry in~~   And in Plato's teeth
&times; That the Greeks lied in the throat

X Declare that there had been naught
   Cry that there was naught
X ~~But~~ ~~Until~~ Till ~~made~~ man has made the whole
149 ~~Made stock and~~ Till man made up the whole
X ~~Made~~ ~~Aye~~ Lock and stock and barrel
151 Out of his bitter soul
   Made sun, and moon and stars all
   And all that is under the sun
X I mock at Greek and Jew
   Why could no Rabbi say

[Yeats has placed a line with a query beside the two lines above.]

   That Eternal Man
   Rested the seventh day
X That day by day we renew
   I mock at Greek and Jew
   And add to what I have said
   Day by day we renew
   The living and the dead

[Facing page 3]
   ~~Of~~ The bursting fruit, ~~or~~ ~~the falling~~ the sudden shower
X The moon full and high
X Out of a summer sky
   Out of a sullen sky
   The swan that in that hour
   When he must fix his eye
141 Upon a fading gleam
   ~~And~~ Float ~~up~~ out up the long
X Glittering stretch of stream
X And there sing his last song
   Last glittering stretch of the stream
144 And there sing his last song
   ~~Or the burst~~ Of bursting fruit, or the sudden shower
   Out of a summer sky
   Of the swan in that last hour
   When he must fix his eye
141 Upon a fading gleam
   And mount ~~his last~~ up a long

143 Last/ Reach of glittering stream
144 And there sing his last song

[The entire page above is cancelled]

[Page 4]

121 It is time that I wrote my will
122 I choose upstanding men
    That climb to pool or rill
    In mountain rocks and at dawn
    Drop their fly at the side
    Of a dripping stone. I declare
127 They shall inherit my pride
    The pride of the people that were
    Bound neither to cause or state
130 Neither to slaves that were spat on
131 Nor to the tyrants that spat
    Those of the people of Grattan
133 That gave though free to refuse:
    A pride like that of the morn
    That lets the wild light loose
136 Or that of the fabulous horn
    Or that of a sudden shower
138 When all streams are dry
139 Or that of the hour
140 When the swan must fix his eye
141 Upon a fading gleam
142 Float out upon a long
143 Last reach of glittering stream
144 And there sing his last song.

[Facing page 4]
    That climbs the streams until
    ~~Rock~~ The weed grown rock, and at dawn
    Drops a cast at the side
    Of a dripping stone

[Page 5]

145 And I declare my faith
146 I mock Plotinus' thought
147 And cry in Plato's teeth

148 Death and life were not
149 Till man made up the whole
~~Aye~~  Made lock and stock and barrel
151 Out of his bitter soul
Aye sun and moon and stars all
153 And further add to that
✕ We ~~made~~  make who is born
We stretch beyond the tomb
And day by day create
Our

[From here on the page has been cancelled]

✕ [undeciphered line]
✕ And then I mock at the Jew
Because ~~he did so say~~  no Rabbi says
That the Eternal Man
Rested the seventh day
✕ And add to what I have said
~~I therein mock at~~  I have great scorn of the Jew
And add to what I have said
That day by day we renew
✕ The living and dead
✕ The blessed dream of the dead
The blessed life/ dream of the dead
With that we make and do
✕ Because their life is a dream
✕ For man and dreams at the last

[Facing page 5]
mind I have made
But ~~of late I have made~~
&
No further I add to that
✕ ~~That~~   ~~And~~   This mockery of the tomb
✕ That living men create
✕ Their own eternal home

F
And

When I go to my final rest
I shall

&times; For dead we are that we made [?]
&times; Or that we have done, and I


[Page 6]
&times; The blessed dream of the dead
&times; And mine [?] is almost ready
&times; The forms come crowding fast
&times; [undeciphered line]
&times; Man is a dream at the last
&times; I ~~make~~ [word undeciphered] ~~peace my peace~~  build my
    learned peace
&times; Poets and saints and kings
&times; Of England Italy Greece
160&times; Poet's imaginings
161&times; And memories of love
162&times; Memories of the words of women
&times; All/ And all those things whereof
&times; ~~They make up their~~  The dead compose superhuman
&times; Mirror resembling dreams
  ~~So~~  And at the loophole there
167 The daws chatter and scream
   And lay twigs layer upon layer
&times; That mount from the stone floor up
&times; To the narrow sill when abreast
&times; They will hollow and round the top
&times; When sill and top are abreast
&times; They will hollow the top
&times; And round it out a nest

[This page in two columns, left given above, right below.]

&times; I build my Eternal peace
&times; With old Italian things
&times; Or the old stones of Greece
160&times; Poet's imaginings

&times; I build my eternal peace,
&times; With stories of dead kings

✕ ~~The~~   In Ireland ~~Italy or~~   or in Greece
✕ Out of Italian Art
✕ Out of the sculpture of Greece

157 I have prepared my peace
     With old Italian things
     And the old stones of Greece
160 Poet's imaginings
161 And memories of love
162 Memories of the words of women
     And all those things whereof
164 ~~The dead create~~   Man makes a superhuman
165 Mirror resembling dream

169 When they have mounted up
170 The mother bird will rest
     Upon their hollow top
✕ And [word undeciphered] her [word undeciphered] nest
     And round their wild nest

[Facing page 6]
     And further add to that
✕ That even being made ["dead" intended?], we rise
✕ And from our acts create
✕ The second Paradise

     ~~That~~   We on the third
     That being dead we
     ~~Men on the third~~   day rise
✕ And if they will
155 Dream and so create
     A second Paradise

[Page 7]
     Yes to young men I leave all
     Pride and faith, to young men
     That ride upon horses and climb the water course
     In grey Connemara cloth
     That cast fly [in] the eddying foam high up the mountain
     Ready for trumpet or beckoning hand
     Message or challenge

I leave them my pride and faith
X  I leave to sanguine men
X  Ready for
X  That want a ~~beckoning hand~~    a summoning [?] blast
X  And care not for a [word undeciphered]
X  Or beckoning hand and blast
   I leave to men that cast
   A summoning blast or hand
   The [word undeciphered] to sanguine men
   [undeciphered partial line]

[Page 8]

   I blow a trumpet blast
   I raise a beckoning hand

X  I make
X  I have called with the sound
X  And raised a beckoning hand
X  To cast their flies at dawn

   My musical notes are blown
   My beckoning hand is raised

[Page 9]

   To young and sanguine men
X  That climb that climb the river
   In grey Connemara cloth
   That drop their flies at dawn
   Among the eddying froth

X  I leave

   I have left faith and pride
X  To young and sanguine men
X  That climb the mountain side
X  To men that near the dawn
   The men that climb at dawn
   The mountain's rocky side
   To young and sanguine men
   In grey Connemara cloth
X  That drop a cast of flies
X  In the eddy and the froth

That drop a cast of flies
Into the eddying froth

I leave to live vigourous men
X That ri climb the riv
That climb the river side
To young and sanguine men
That find ~~where the~~

[Facing page 9]
Young/ May young and sanguine men
X In grey Connemara cloth
That climb up near the dawn
To drop in eddying froth
A deft cast of flies
In a cleft mountain side
Under the cold skies
Inherit my faith and pride

To men who climb at dawn
The rocky river's source
To young and sanguine men
That find the river's source

[This page in two columns, left given above, right below.]

I left to vigourous men
Not sedentary as I
To

That climb the river course
X That they cast/ fling near dawn
That they stand at dawn
X Where the cold source
X Under the
To find their high source
X Under the
~~In~~ Under bursting dawn
In the cleft mountain side
To young and sanguine men
My faith and my pride

[Page 10]

They climb the river courses
In grey Connemara cloth
Up to where the source is
Amid its eddying froth
And cast a line as dawn
Breaks on the mountain side
&times; A vigourous healthy man
&times; I ~~bid~~   call these vigourous men
&times; Inherit
&times; To inherit faith and pride
I beckon to these men
And offer faith and pride

I ~~leave~~   have left ~~both~~   faith and pride
&times; To ~~vigourous sanguine~~   young vigourous
&times; To these upstanding men
175 That climb the mountain side
~~That~~   under the bursting dawn
That they may drop a fly
Being of like metal made
179 Till ~~Though~~   it was broken by
180 This sedentary trade

[Facing page 10]

That traverse/ tread the river courses
In grey Connemara cloth
Up to where the source is
Amid the eddying froth

&times; Many men
That climb the river courses
&times; Up the cleft mountain side
&times; And tell us where the source is

They tread
~~Men climb~~   the river courses
In grey Connemara cloth

        dawn
        side
        men
        pride

> And cast their lines ~~at~~   as the dawn
> ~~In the cleft~~   Breaks on mountain side
> Young and sanguine men
> Inherit my ~~pride~~   faith and pride

Section III of "The Tower" grows out of these lines in section I:

> It seems that I must bid the Muse go pack,
> Choose Plato and Plotinus for a friend
> Until imagination, ear and eye,
> Can be content with argument and deal
> In abstract things; or be derided by
> A sort of battered kettle at the heel.

The general subject of section III is Yeats's refusal to take the course of action here anticipated. Instead he chooses for his heirs men like the "freckled man" he had imagined as being an ideal audience in "The Fisherman," and then composes a poetic last will and testament in which he leaves his heirs the Anglo-Irish pride he has himself embodied. He goes on to reject Plato and Plotinus —

> I mock Plotinus' thought
> And cry in Plato's teeth —

before declaring his own esoteric faith. Then, amusedly aware, perhaps, of the somewhat ramshackle nature of this "faith" as compared with Judaism and Christianity, he composes the delightful image of the daw's nest — a daw's nest is a mere heap of trash which yet serves life's obscure purpose well enough. He leaves this faith to his imagined heirs and then claims kinship with them.

Presumably Yeats had this general arrangement in mind when he started to write, though not the exact relation of the parts. Once he establishes relation, the floundering on pages 1, 2, and 3 becomes a sudden assurance on page 4. He had also decided to use a metrical pattern different from those used in sections I and II. Section I is in five stress lines which rhyme alternately; section II uses the elaborate stanza which Yeats had earlier used in "Prayer for my Daughter" and "In Memory of Major Robert Gregory," and was to use again in "Byzantium"; section III returns to the rhyme scheme of I, but the stresses have been reduced to three. In the earliest drafts there is some hesitation between four-stress and three-stress lines ("Under a dark stone/

Under the edge of a dark stone"), but soon the metrical pattern Yeats kept emerges.

In manuscript pages 1 and 2 Yeats has immense difficulty with the lines describing the heir or heirs he has chosen, and his difficulties return with his heirs' return at lines 173–80. I will consider possible explanations of these difficulties when we get to these lines, but want to deal with one part of the problem here. Part of the trouble comes, I think, because Yeats returns to "The Fisherman" to find the kind of man he wants for heir. I have noticed time after time how difficult it was for Yeats to make a new beginning; prose subjects and early drafts of poems are frequently haunted by echoes of work already finished. An example of this is found in the "Creed" on which "Under Ben Bulben" was based (see part i of introduction to "Poems"). Section ii of this "Creed" shows that Yeats considered using the image of Sato's sword once again, an image he had already used many times. While composing lines 122–26 and 173–80 of "The Tower" Yeats considered direct references to, and verbal echoes of "The Fisherman": "And chose once, that tall young man"; "sunflecked," and "grey Connemara cloth." In the final versions of both passages Yeats has reduced his allusions to the earlier poem to a pleasant echo. While adjusting this difficulty, Yeats also generalized his setting by abandoning references to Ben Bulben and Ochte. The difficulty of making a beginning is shown by the fact that at the end of the second page Yeats has not written any lines he will keep, and has only one line end in place ("dawn," line 124).

In the drafts Yeats now goes on to his declaration of faith; the idea of stating his own and Anglo-Irish pride and willing it to his heirs developed later. The many drafts of this declaration of faith (lines 145–65) are of great interest, for they show that in the 1920's although Yeats was questioning Christian doctrines as he had questioned them before ("The Magi") and would again in many poems which culminate in "Supernatural Songs," he was not questioning them very openly. "Two Songs from a Play" seem an exception, but perhaps Yeats felt these poems were so gnomic and learned they would not offend. I see, perhaps fancifully, in these revisions an effort to spare Irish sensibilities, which, given the whole record, seems rather odd. Perhaps Yeats remembered that an Irish senator was writing "The Tower," perhaps he is simply conscious of the fact that he is directly addressing an Irish audience. On manuscript page 3 it is not the God of Genesis who rested on the seventh day of the creation, but "Eternal Man." As the drafts proceed Yeats softens his statements that man has created this world and the next by enveloping them in a kind of esoteric fog. Here he even drops all reference to Jewish tradition, which he once rejected along with the Greek. In these early drafts of his declaration of faith Yeats develops a line of thought he was to keep, makes a good start at establishing his rhyme [2] sounds, and composes four lines that still stand (145, 146, 149, 151).

Then on the facing page Yeats begins work on his statement of Anglo-Irish pride (lines 126–44). He gropes his way, as it were, toward the images he will use to characterize this pride: the shower and swan images are in place, and "bursting fruit" perhaps anticipates the "fabulous horn" of the finished poem. Eight rhyme sounds and seven rhyme words are in place; three lines are finished.

On manuscript page 4 Yeats puts the fisherman and his legacy of pride together, thereby getting the first twenty-four lines of section III pretty well organized, though he later improved them greatly by verbal revision. All the rhyme sounds are in place, and all save one of the rhyme words (line 123); fourteen lines are in final form. It was at this point, no doubt, that Yeats cancelled the page facing 3.

On manuscript page 5 and on the facing page Yeats returns to his declaration of faith and gets lines 145–53 into shape. It was while working on this draft, apparently, that Yeats decided to cut his references to Jewish tradition and Eternal Man. All the rhyme words are established, and seven lines are finished. The words he needs to state the esoteric doctrine of lines 154–56 continue to elude Yeats, perhaps because he is not quite sure what his "faith" about the life after death is.

On the sixth manuscript page, after another abortive try at lines 154–56, Yeats continues the poem with a first draft of lines 157–72. Yeats has written all over this page. From internal evidence I deduce that he wrote the material in this order: the lines in the left column were composed first, and in order; the right column was used for rewriting, but the material there is not in the order of composition. The five lines "I build my eternal peace . . . Out of the sculpture of Greece" were written before the lines just above them "I build my Eternal peace . . . Poet's imaginings." Then, still in the right column, beginning "I have prepared my peace," Yeats drafted lines 157–65 in nearly final form; he picked up the three uncancelled lines in the left column beginning "And at the loophole there," and completed his draft of lines 166–72 in the right column. If one reads only the uncancelled lines on this manuscript page, he will discover that Yeats has this part of the poem pretty well shaped up. He has written the same number of lines he will use in the finished poem, the rhyme sounds are all in place, and nine lines are finished. Yeats appears to have achieved the happy image of the daw's nest very quickly and directly.

On the manuscript page facing 6 Yeats has a final try at lines 154–56. While doing this, he states another heresy, this one quickly abandoned. Earlier he had assigned to creative man God's role in Genesis; here he equates creative man with Christ when he writes:

Men on the third day rise
Dream and so create
A second Paradise.

This certainly is a clearer statement of doctrine than the ultimate lines

That, being dead, we rise,
Dream and so create
Translunar Paradise.

Manuscript pages 7, 8, 9, and 10, along with such facing pages as Yeats wrote on, were all used to draft what are now lines 173–80. Yeats makes many false starts; he has some trouble managing his persona, for he sounds pompous and affected when he writes

I blow a trumpet blast
I raise a beckoning hand.

He has more trouble reintroducing his fisherman heir than he had introducing him earlier in the drafts. When Yeats got stuck during the process of composition, he really got stuck. There are always signs of such trouble, one of them being the physical appearance of the writing. On page 7, for instance, the writing trails off into an indecipherable scrawl, as though Yeats knew while writing that he wasn't getting anything he could use. Finally on page 10 Yeats breaks through the impasse after a series of attacks and very nearly achieves the lines he was to keep.

One can only speculate why these lines and lines 122–26 proved so difficult. I should like to start by observing a marked similarity between section III of "The Tower" and "Under Ben Bulben." Both contain declarations of faith; both are addressed to Yeats's spiritual heirs. In theme the poems are very much alike, but in tone very unlike. In "Under Ben Bulben" Yeats invites all forthcoming poets, sculptors, and painters to

> Bring the soul of man to God,
> Make him fill the cradles right.

Later in the poem he is more particular when he writes:

> Irish poets, learn your trade. . . .
> Cast your mind on other days
> That we in coming days may be
> Still the indomitable Irishry.[3]

Here Yeats knows precisely who his heirs are (artists who come after him), and he knows precisely what he wants them to do: they are to carry on the tradition in art within which he himself has worked. In "The Tower" Yeats has a very difficult time deciding what qualities he wants in his heirs. They are not as in "Under Ben Bulben" to be artists who will succeed him: we conclude rather from the allusions to "The Fisherman" that they are to form an imagined ideal audience for his own work. By the time he finishes Yeats has decided that they are to be men of action rather than men of thought, hence the fishing and mountain climbing; they are to embody his and Irish pride derived from intellectuals and patriots of that eighteenth-century Ireland which Yeats was making into a myth; they are to be men who can receive his here vaguely stated non-Christian faith.

If we assemble the successive versions of lines 122 and 174, we will be able to pinpoint Yeats's difficulties:

122 And choose for an heir young men and tall
And chose once, that tall young man
Some tall young man shall be my heir
And chose a sunflecked man for an heir
I choose a tall young man for an heir
I choose a stalwart man for my heir
I choose young outstanding men
I choose upstanding men

174 Yes to young men I leave all
I leave to sanguine men

To young and sanguine men
I leave to live vigourous men
May young and sanguine men
I left to vigourous men
To young and sanguine men
A vigourous healthy man
I call these vigourous men
To vigourous sanguine [men]
To young vigourous [men]
To these upstanding men
Young and sanguine men
To young upstanding men

[This last line is from the MS. dated Oct. 7, 1925.]

The drafts of line 122 show, I think, that in trying to conceive of his valid heirs Yeats was far from sure just what qualities he wanted them to have. Should they merely be young men of good physique, or should they have certain moral qualities, and, if so, what moral qualities? Yeats starts with the merely physical. "Young men and tall" has no real content, and so it is eventually rejected for the visual, the primitive "sunflecked." Despite "The Fisherman" this fails to suggest the kind of continuity Yeats seeks for himself. Physical and ethical qualities combine in "stalwart," but the word is far too hackneyed for serious poetry, so Yeats backs off from it into something worse, the Rotarian "young outstanding." The sound of this suggests a solution. "Upstanding" works, after a fashion, for it does combine the physical and ethical (OED "of open, honest or independent bearing" "having an erect carriage, well set up"), and it is not hackneyed. In the drafts of line 174 Yeats explores the possibility of using three other adjectives — "sanguine," "vigourous," "healthy" — again rather hackneyed ones, but finally decides to stick with "upstanding." While "upstanding" beautifully characterizes Yeats's own and Anglo-Irish pride, it fails to suggest either the effects or ends of that pride. Since it does so fail, Yeats seems in these passages neither to know himself nor his heirs; "upstanding" is a merely verbal solution. In short, I suggest that the difficulty Yeats experienced in composing these lines grew out of his uncertainty about what he wanted to say. Section III of "The Tower" excels in rejecting, in mocking Plotinus' thought and crying in Plato's teeth. But its characterization of Anglo-Irish pride sounds a little strident until Yeats gets to images, and he narrowly escapes the hackneyed, even the maudlin, when he chooses and describes his heirs and his own relation to them.

Hard as all this was, one of Yeats's best lines, "This sedentary trade," seems to have come quite easily. The word "sedentary" first appears in the right column on the page facing 9 where Yeats writes "Not sedentary as I." Then, at the bottom of page 10, Yeats struck off his splendid line without any more experimenting.

When he had finished these drafts, Yeats was well on his way to finishing section III of "The Tower." We can follow his progress further in a manuscript of the entire poem which Yeats finished October 7, 1925, and in TS. 1 and TS. 2. In the manuscript section III goes as follows:

```
121  It is time that I wrote my will:
122  I choose upstanding men
123  That climb the streams until
  ✕  The reed grown
124  The last   The fountain leap and at dawn
125  Drop their cast at the side
     Of a dripping stone. I declare
127  They shall inherit my pride:
128  The pride of the people that were
     Bound neither to cause or state
130  Neither to slaves that were spat on
131  Nor to the tyrants that spat
  ✕  Those of the people of Grattan
     John Synge and those people of Grattan
133  That gave though free to refuse,
134  Pride like that of the morn
     Casting its strange light loose
136  Or that of the fabulous horn
     Or that of a sudden shower
138  When all streams are dry
139  Or that of the hour
140  When the swan must fix his eye
141  Upon a fading gleam
142  Float out upon a long
143  Last reach of glittering stream
144  And there sing his last song.
```

145  And I declare my faith:
146  I mock Plotinus' thought
147  And cry in Plato's teeth
148  Death and life were not
149  Till man made up the whole
      Made lock and stock and barrel
151  Out of his bitter soul
      Aye sun and moon and stars all,
153  And further add to that
154  That being dead we rise
155  Dream and so create
      A second Paradise
157  I have prepared my peace
158  With learned Italian things
159  And the proud stones of Greece
160  Poet's imaginings
161  And memories of love
162  Memories of the words of women
      And all those things whereof
164  Man makes a superhuman
165  Mirror resembling dream;
      I have left faith and pride
174  To young upstanding men
175  That climb the mountain side
      That under the bursting dawn
177  They may drop a fly,
178  Being of that metal made
179  Till it was broken by
180  This sedentary trade.
                   Sept Oct 1925

At this point Yeats has altered the end of the poem by omitting the
extended simile of the daw's nest. On October 7 he decided to rein-
state that passage. He cancelled lines 173–80 and added another page
to his MS. which goes as follows:

166  And at the loophole there
167  The daws chatter and scream
168  And drop twigs — layer upon layer
169  When it has   they have mounted up

170 The mother bird will rest
171 ~~Upon~~ On their hollow top
    And warm her wild nest.

173 I leave both faith and pride
174 To young upstanding men
175 That climb the mountain side
176 That under bursting dawn
177 They may drop a fly;
178 Being of that metal made
179 Till it was broken by
180 This sedentary trade.

WBY. ~~Sept~~ Oct 7 1925

When this version of section III is compared with the earlier drafts, we find that Yeats has completed lines 123–25, 128, 134, 154, 158–59, 166, 171, 173–74, 176–78. None of the changes is substantive; they involve minor adjustments of diction and meter. Section III of "The Tower" in TS. 1 is verbally identical with the MS. just printed. Yeats corrected a carbon copy of TS. 1 and made the following changes in wording:

John Synge and those people of Grattan
That of those people of Grattan
132 The people of Burke and of Grattan

and

Casting its strange light loose
135 When the headlong light is loose.

All Yeats's lines are now in the form first printed except lines 126, 129, 137, 150, 152, 156, 163, and 172; these require such slight changes as the dropping or adding of a single syllable, as in line 172 where

And warm her wild nest

becomes

And so warm her wild nest.

There is evidence in this same copy of TS. 1 that Yeats was still not satisfied with the end of the poem, for he has cancelled lines 173–80. These lines are omitted from TS. 2, where Yeats has added lines

181–95 with which the poem we know ends. No manuscript versions of these new lines have been found, so I cannot trace the history of their composition. Apparently Yeats completed them in 1926, the date he gave the finished poem. All the lines of "The Tower" section III which are included in TS. 2 are in the form first printed except line 156. Before Yeats printed the poem he returned lines 173–80 to its text.

## ii

### "Lullaby"

YEATS WROTE THE EARLY DRAFTS of "Lullaby," and many other poems included in "Words for Music Perhaps," in the Rapallo Notebook inscribed "Diary of Thought begun Sept 23. 1928 in Dublin." Yeats was in Rapallo when he wrote the poem, away from his Dublin study. Very often when Yeats was away from home he used a bound manuscript book as a workbook, as in this instance. "Lullaby" is a different kind of poem from those we have been studying. Yeats deeply loved the poem and lavished on it, I think, even greater care than usual.

[Draft A]
[Page 1, left-hand page of first opening]

> sleep
> alarms
> deep
> bed
> arms

Thus sang
X  A mother sang her child asleep
Thus a mother sang to sleep
X  The child that lay upon her breast
X  Sleep and as deep

~~That~~  Thus a mother sang asleep
The child her breast had fed
Sleep beloved and as deep
As daring Paris did

Sleep beloved sleep
The breast where [you] have fed
X  ~~Protects~~  Must guard you from all ha

Sleep where you have fed
Forget the world's alarms

Sleep upon my breast
As

[Page 2, right-hand page of first opening]

As Paris slept
That first night
In his Helen's arms

The sleep that Paris found
Towards the break of day
Under the slow breaking day
That first night in Helen's arms

That first night on Helen's bed

X  That first
X  Sleep the sleep
   The sleep that dreaming Paris
X  When that morning broke
   That first dawn
   That first sleep that Paris found

[Page 3, left-hand page of second opening. Yeats cancelled this page.]

Sleep beloved sleep
Sleep where you have fed
Forget the world's alarms

Sleep beloved, lie   sink asleep
On the breast where [you] have fed
X  Forgetful of the world's alarms

X  Sleep beloved
X  Sleep, beloved and

   Beloved may you sink as deep
X  As far from fright [?]

X  Sleep beloved sink in sleep

   Put away the world's alarms
   Sink into a rest as deep

[Page 4, right-hand page of second opening. Yeats divided the page by drawing a line.]

  ✕  That sank upon the golden bed
  ✕  When the dawn broke in ~~Helen's~~  arms

  1  Beloved may your sleep be sound
  2  ~~On the breast where you have~~  That have found it where you fed
     What were all the world's alarms
     To that great Paris when he found
     Sleep upon the golden bed
  6  That first dawn in Helen's arms?

— — — — — — — — — — — — — — — — — —

     Sleep beloved with such a sleep
     ~~As that~~  As on the hunter Tristram fell
  ✕  When beloved night had gone
  ✕  When the potion's work was done
  ✕  At the end
  ✕  When the last
  ✕  When at
     When the birds began to stir
     And all the potion's work was done

     Sleep beloved the sleep that fell
     On Tristram the famed forester
     When all the potion's work was done

[Yeats wrote the next two lines on the bottom of page three.]

     Sleep beloved with such sleep
     As the hunter Tristram got

[Page 5, right-hand page of third opening. The drafts on this page are earlier than those on the facing left-hand page.]

  7  Sleep beloved such a sleep
     As Tristram that famed forester felt
  ✕  When the potion ~~had its will~~  will was done
  ✕  Found when
     Found when the potion's work ~~was~~  being done
  ✕  When the birds began
  ✕  Found when birds began to stir

&times; When the deer began to
&times; When

&times; And bird could sing and nestling cheep
&times; And stag
&times; Birds could sing and
   Birds could warble, deer could leap
   The oak leaf and the beech leaf stir
   And the world begin again

[Page 6, left-hand page of third opening. Yeats has divided the page by drawing a line.]

&times; Lie beloved fast asleep
 7 Sleep beloved such a sleep
   As Tristram that famed forester
&times; Found when the potion's work was done/ being done
   Found when the potion's work being done
&times; Birds could sing, and
   The birds could sing, the deer could leap
   The oak bough and the beech bough stir
   And the world begin again

— — — — — — — — — — — — — — — — — —

Found the potion's work being done
When birds could sing and deer could leap
bank               swan

sank               bank
love               ~~limbs~~

         swan     sank
         dims     care

         limbs

[Page 7, right-hand page of fourth opening. Yeats used the left-hand page for rewriting. Passages from the left-hand page have been worked into the drafts where they seem to belong. Yeats worked on stanzas 2 and 3 on this page, perhaps simultaneously. I have separated them.]

   Such sleep, as on Eurota's bank
&times; Did the famous Leda guard
&times; Where
&times; Did the king of heaven guard

[From the left-hand page.]

$\times$  Such sleep as Leda tried to guard
$\times$  When upon Eurota's bank
                    bank
                    where
                    length
                    sank
                    care

[Continues on the right-hand page.]

    ~~Sleep~~  Belovéd such a sleep as fell
14  ~~On~~  Upon Eurota's grassy bank
15  When the holy ~~swan~~  bird that ~~swan~~  there
16  Accomplished ~~the~~  his predestined will
17  From the limbs of Leda sank
18  But not from her protecting care

[From the left-hand page.]

    Such a sleep as Leda saw
    When upon Eurota's bank
                              where
                              care

[Continues on the right-hand page.]

$\times$  Lie beloved ~~fast asleep~~  in such a sleep
7  Sleep belovéd such a sleep
8  ~~Such~~  As did that wild Tristram know
9  When the potion's work being done
    ~~The~~  Birds could sing ~~the~~  and deer could leap
    The beech bough sway and the oak bough
    And the world begin again

    Stag could run ~~crop~~  and hares could leap
    Birds could sing and stags could leap
$\times$  And pheasants crow upon the bough
$\times$  For the world began again
    The beech bough sway by the oak bough
    And the world begin again

[Draft B]

## LULLABY

### I

1 Beloved may your sleep be sound
2 That have found it where you fed
   What were all the world's alarms
&times; To that great Paris when he found
&times; What to Paris when he found
   To mighty Paris when he found
   Sleep upon the golden bed
6 That first dawn in Helen's arms

### II

7 Sleep beloved such a sleep
8 As did that wild Tristram know
9 When the potion's work ~~was~~ being done
   ~~Stage~~ Stag could run and ~~hares~~ roe could leap
   The beech bough sway by the oak bough
&times; And the world begin again
   Stag could leap and roe could run

### III

   Beloved such a sleep as fell
14 Upon Eurota's grassy bank
15 When the holy ~~swan~~ bird that there
16 Accomplished his predestined will
17 From the limbs of Leda sank
18 But not from her protecting care

          March 1929

[Yeats wrote another draft of this poem on a separate sheet; here the poem reaches the form in which it was first printed in *The New Keepsake*.]

[Draft C]

## ~~CRADLE SONG~~
## LULLABY

1 Beloved may your sleep be sound
2 That have found it where you fed.
3 What are all the world's alarms?
4 What were they when Paris found

5 Sleep upon a golden bed
6 That first dawn in Helen's arms.

7 Sleep beloved such a sleep
8 As did that wild Tristram know
9 When, the potion's work being done,
10 Roe could run or doe could leap
11 Under ~~the~~  oak and ~~the hazel~~  beechen bough,
12 Roe could leap or doe could run;

13 Such a sleep, and sound as fell
14 Upon Eurota's grassy bank
15 When the holy bird, that there
16 Accomplished his predestined will,
17 From the limbs of Leda sank
18 But not from her protecting care.

Yeats has his usual trouble getting "Lullaby" started; as the drafts continue he proceeds more and more surely until he accomplishes a finished draft of stanza three the first time he attempts it. Yeats seems from the first to be working toward a six-line stanza, though he does experiment with different rhyme schemes and line lengths. He seems also to have his three extended allusions to the love stories of Paris, Tristram, and Zeus established in his mind.

Yeats begins his work on stanza 1 by listing five possible rhyme words. These are not arranged in the scheme he eventually adopted (abcabc), but he does use three of the five — alarms, bed, arms — in the finished poem. Then Yeats sets the scene, so to speak, by writing

Thus a mother sang to sleep
The child that lay upon her breast.

On page 1 of the drafts he drops this indirect approach in favor of having the whole poem a song when he writes

Sleep beloved sleep
Sleep where you have fed.

In the drafts on pages 1, 2, and 3 the third line is addressed to the child as it again will be in the C draft, and it is put through many revisions while being transferred to sleeping Paris on page 4. Yeats then goes on to work out his comparison of the sleeping child with Paris asleep on Helen's bed after their first night together. On page 2 this is stated simply:

> As Paris slept
> That first night
> In his Helen's arms

Then Yeats remembers that though the world speaks of lovers sleeping together that is not what the world means, so he immediately changes his expression to a more accurate one:

> The sleep that Paris found
> Towards the break of day
> That first night on Helen's bed.

By the end of page 2 Yeats has not finished any lines, and he has not certainly established his rhyme scheme; though five rhyme words are in place they are not in final order (fed, alarms, found, arms, bed).

The draft on page 3 is still hesitating and uncertain, Yeats does not make much progress. Then on page 4 the first stanza takes shape. Yeats finishes lines 1, 2, and 6 and nearly finishes the others. The slight but wonderfully effective changes Yeats makes can be seen by comparing this draft with the latest forms of the various lines in the preceding drafts:

1  Beloved may you sink as deep
   Beloved may your sleep be sound
2  On the breast where [you] have fed
   That have found it where you fed
3  Put away the world's alarms
   What were all the world's alarms
4  That first sleep that Paris found
   To that great Paris when he found
5  That sank upon the golden bed
   Sleep upon the golden bed
6  When the dawn broke in Helen's arms
   That first dawn in Helen's arms?

The revision of line 1 helps Yeats develop his persona, the imagined mother who sings the lullaby: "Beloved may you sink as deep" is truer to the object; "Beloved may your sleep be sound" is truer to the persona, since it expresses her wish rather than merely an observation.

On the lower half of page 4 Yeats begins work on stanza 2, continuing on 5 and the top half of 6; his progress is much faster. Yeats selects and arranges the detail which will convey Tristram sleeping in the waking forest after the consummation of his love. Line 7 reaches final form on page 5; in the drafts of line 8 "hunter Tristram" becomes "Tristram that famed forester." Line 9 throughout these drafts has the same content, but goes through many verbal changes: "When beloved night had gone/ When the potion's work was done/ And all the potion's work was done/ When all the potion's work was done/ When the potion's will was done/ Found when the potion's work being done." In the drafts of lines 10–12 Yeats introduces these dawn sounds: stirring, singing, and then warbling birds; leaping deer; stirring oak and beech leaves. At the end of page 5 Yeats has completed line 7 and set the rhyme words for lines 9 and 10. The draft of this stanza on the top of page 6 shows some advance. The birds are now content to sing, and the leaves have become boughs.

On the lower half of page 6 Yeats experiments with rhyme words for stanza 3, and in his right-hand column sets three of the words he will use in the finished poem — bank, sank, care. In the drafts of stanza 3 on page 7 Yeats's attack is both quick and sure. He explores his details a bit, and then writes the stanza off in a single draft, essentially as it appeared in *The New Keepsake*. Yeats then returns to drafts of stanza 2. He finishes lines 7–9; lines 10–12 do not yet come right. Rhyming "done" and "again" seems daring even for Yeats. The dawn birds, who will shortly disappear, are giving trouble.

Draft B, dated March 1929, is little more than a clean copy of the A drafts. Yeats did make changes in lines 4, and 10–12. At line 4 "To that great Paris" becomes "To mighty Paris"; at lines 10–12 Yeats begins to work his way toward his final readings. At the bottom of page 7 of the A drafts lines 10–12 read:

> Birds could sing and stags could leap
> The beech bough sway by the oak bough
> And the world begin again.

Now Yeats banishes the birds, rephrases line 10, cancels line 12 and replaces it by repeating the image used in 10, slightly changing the order of the words:

> Stag could run and roe could leap
> The beech bough sway by the oak bough
> Stag could leap and roe could run.

Yeats has found the strategy though not the words used in the finished poem. A general statement "And the world begin again," summing up the content of the preceding images, is dropped in favor of a refrain-like repetition of one of those images. When this happens the slight consonance of *done/ again* becomes full rhyme in *done/ run*. In Yeats's poetry such summary statements of the content of his images as the one here dropped occur frequently:

> Mere anarchy is loosed upon the world

for example, or

> Those masterful images because complete
> Grew in pure mind, but out of what began?

Yeats must have felt that such a statement was not necessary in this simple poem; perhaps too it had the effect of somewhat removing our attention from the sleeping lovers.

In draft C "Lullaby" reached the form in which *The New Keepsake* first printed it in November 1931. Here Yeats changes the wording of lines 3, 4, 10–12, and 13.

> What were all the world's alarms
> To mighty Paris when he found

> 3 What are all the world's alarms?
> 4 What were they when Paris found

> Stag could run and roe could leap
> The beech bough sway by the oak bough
> Stag could leap and roe could run
> 10 Roe could run or doe could leap
> 11 Under oak and beechen bough,
> 12 Roe could leap or doe could run

> Beloved such a sleep as fell
> 13 Such a sleep, and sound as fell

Here line 3 again becomes a question asked of the sleeping child, a form of it I like, though Yeats eventually reverted to the reading found in the B draft. Line 4 in its new wording introduces the first allusion neatly and avoids "mighty Paris," which rather jars on the ears of readers of the *Iliad*. The changes in the second stanza accomplish several things: they introduce what is to my ear a very insistent internal rhyme; they soften the sound by deleting "stag" — there is now a ripe interplay of soft consonants and open vowels; they change the boughs from a correlative to the mere setting of a correlative — they had been one of the images set to show us the reawakening forest, now they describe the place where the deer leap and run. The new form of line 13 was invented, I think, to avoid a third repetition of "beloved"; Yeats achieves a more subtle variation of line 1 when he drops "beloved" and picks up "sound."

As was noted above the draft just discussed is exactly that first printed in *The New Keepsake*. It would be easy enough to move from this first printing to the final text of the poem which was established in Macmillan's *Winding Stair* in 1933. It would only be necessary to say that in 1933 Yeats reverted to the form lines 3 and 4 had in draft B, keeping the rest of the poem as it had been printed. But between these two printings came the version printed in the Cuala Press's *Words for Music* in November 1932. Since I propose to discuss this version in detail, I print it below:

LULLABY

Beloved may your sleep be sound
That have found it where you fed.
What were all the world's alarms
To mighty Paris when he found
Sleep upon a golden bed
That first night in Helen's arms.

Sleep beloved such a sleep
As did that wild Tristram know
When, the potion's work being done,
Stag could run and roe leap
Under oak and beeches bough,
Stag could leap and roe could run.

Beloved such a sleep as fell
Upon Eurotas' grassy bank
When the holy bird that there

> Accomplished his predestined will
> From the limbs of Helen sank
> But not from her protecting care.

I shall first describe the relationship of the three earliest printings, and then speculate concerning their relationship. I assume that the following Cuala Press readings are misprints which I may ignore: line 11 "beeches bough," line 17 "From the limbs of Helen sank"; and further that "Eurota's" in line 14 of the *New Keepsake* text derives from the copy Yeats supplied and that the change to the correct form in the Cuala Press version need not be further discussed. If these assumptions are allowed, then the three versions have identical forms of lines 1, 2, 5, 7–9, 11, 14–16; *New Keepsake* and Macmillan identical forms of lines 6, 10, 12, 13; Cuala Press and Macmillan identical forms of lines 3 and 4.

Now for speculation. The Cuala Press text of "Lullaby" seems to me very poor for several reasons. First, because of the misprints already noted: "Under oak and beeches bough" is bad enough, but the confusion of Helen with Leda in line 17 quite spoils the poem. Then the form line 6 has in the Cuala Press printing

> That first night in Helen's arms

reintroduces a reading Yeats had abandoned on page 2 of the A drafts, abandoned, that is, very early in the process of composing the poem. Not only does the reading "first dawn" wonderfully set the stage for stanza 2 by a typical Yeatsean preparation for the emergence of a new correlative, it is also more accurate and avoids the initial but here unwanted association most readers will have with the phrase "first night," namely a first production of a dramatic work.

It is difficult to imagine how such a version got into print a full year after a satisfactory text had appeared. One must, I think, conclude that Cuala printed from very poor copy, from some early and superseded version of the poem, perhaps from a typescript which Yeats had not corrected. Since the poem had been virtually finished in March 1929, there were undoubtedly many copies of it about in 1932. One would go on to conclude that when Yeats prepared copy for Macmillan he kept the *New Keepsake* readings for all lines except 3 and 4; for these he preferred the Cuala Press readings. The poem in its final form is, then, a corrected, eclectic text.

Whether Yeats's art was greatest in the 1920's or the 1930's is a question like the question whether Burgundy is better than claret, Rhine better than Mosel; and we, Yeats's readers, are in the position of the French judge who, when asked to adjudicate between Burgundy and claret, replied that he was willing to spend his life examining the evidence, but that he did not expect to reach a conclusion. It is impossible, I think, to do more than prefer "Nineteen Hundred and Nineteen" to "Supernatural Songs," or "Supernatural Songs" to "Nineteen Hundred and Nineteen." In the 1920's the prevailing mode in Yeats's poetry is the "public speech" mode; he then wrote many poems in his role of vatic poet commenting on men and events in a rhetoric that is traditional, noble, and in some degree forensic. In the 1930's the prevailing mode is metaphysical in the philosophic sense of that word; typical poems are concerned with final things, and Yeats's rhetoric is often fantastic ("Supernatural Songs") and even at times outrageous ("News for the Delphic Oracle"). Yet the prevailing modes barely prevail; Yeats wrote metaphysical poems in the 1920's ("Two Songs from a Play"), public speech poems in the 1930's ("Lapis Lazuli"). Both sorts of poem are now in their different ways usually personal utterances. Yeats found this approach congenial and, once he had established it, rarely tried another.

Both sorts of poem are more and more concerned with Yeats's central doctrine, Unity of Being; they are, so to speak, variations on this theme. The doctrine, Unity of Being, developed so slowly that it is difficult to set a date when it was clearly enough formulated to be operative in Yeats's poetry. The year 1919 will do as well as any; in that year Yeats wrote in "If I were Four-and-Twenty" [first printed in *The Living Age*, Oct. 4, 1919, p. 33]:

When Dr. Hyde delivered in 1894 his lecture on the necessity of 'the de-anglicization of Ireland,' to a society that was a youthful indiscretion of my own, I heard an enthusiastic hearer say: 'This lecture begins a new epoch in Ireland.' It did that, and if I were not four-and-fifty, with no settled habit but the writing of verse, rheumatic, indolent, discouraged, and about to move to the Far East, I would begin another epoch by recommending to the nation a new doctrine, that of unity of being.

By one of those pleasant ironies which abound in Yeats's career, he did not move to the Far East; he ignored his rheumatism, indolence, discouragement; he spent the next twenty years recommending the new doctrine.

# POEMS

## WRITTEN IN THE 1930's

*i*

## "The Mother of God"

ON NOVEMBER 23, 1930, Yeats made the first entry in a new manuscript book, by far the largest and most sumptuous he ever used. He continued to work in this book into the summer of 1933. In it he composed drafts of many of the poems included in *The Winding Stair*, among them "The Mother of God" and "Vacillation." Yeats was staying at Coole during most of the fall and winter of 1931–32, in order to be with Lady Gregory during her final illness. Both poems were composed during these months.

The subject of "The Mother of God," along with the subject of "Remorse for Intemperate Speech" and some notes on Cowley's rhymes, is found in this same book, near the end of a manuscript draft of *The Resurrection*. One would like to conclude from this that the idea of the poem occurred to Yeats while he was at work on the play, and possibly this happened. The question whether Christ was man, or God, or both man and God is the substance of the play. Mary's attitude towards Christ's divinity is discussed in it. But Yeats seldom used his bound manuscript books methodically, starting on page 1 and going to the end; indeed his use of this particular book was decidedly unmethodical. Since it is certain that the items in the book do not occur in order of their composition, it seems more probable that Yeats skipped a page while composing draft 3 of *The Resurrection*, and filled it in later with various notes, including the subject of "The Mother of God." Certainly the poem was written after Yeats completed draft 3 of *The Resurrection*; indeed the finished play was being printed by the Cuala Press at the very time he wrote the poem. Since Yeats usually went on to compose a poem rather soon after writing its subject, I am inclined to think that the subject as well as the poem itself is later than *The Resurrection*.

Here is the subject:

The Virgin shrinks from the annunciation. Must she receive "the burning heavens in her womb"? Looks at the child upon her knees at once "with love and dread."

The quotation marks Yeats placed around the phrases "the burning heavens in her womb" and "with love and dread" no doubt indicated that he intended to use them in the poem. He found a place for the first at the end of stanza 1, the last line of which, in all the drafts as in the finished poem, reads "The Heavens in my womb." The second phrase so marked was not used, but it does express the central idea of the poem. Neither the subject nor the drafts of "The Mother of God" found in the manuscript book are dated. A manuscript on a detached sheet is dated "Sep 3 1931." Mrs. Yeats has dated the composition of the poem September 3–12, 1931. Yeats was at work on the poem before September 3, since the version with that date is clearly later than some of those found in the manuscript book.

When composing a poem in a manuscript book, Yeats often established a center, so to speak, and then worked out from it in both directions. He did this when composing "The Mother of God." The earliest drafts of the poem found in the manuscript book were written in ink. I have arranged these in what I believe to be the order of their composition and called them MS. 1.

### [MS. 1]

X  Threefold the terror that upon me came
X  The terror of the dove in the room
X  The terror that smote me through the ear

X  Terror of the voice out of the air,
X  Terror of the dove in the room,

   ✕  Terror of that that smote me through the ear
   ✕  Terror of the dove in the room

   ✕  Terror of what smote me through the ear
   ✕  Terror of that voice in the air
   ✕  Terror of a dove in the room
   ✕  Terror of all terrors that I bear
5 ✕  The heavens in my womb

   ✕  Past terror
   ✕  Three terrors — the

   ✕  A three fold terror — the light shining there
   ✕  The shaft that struck me in the ear
   ✕  ~~That burst into~~   Bursting through the hollow of an ear
   ✕  The terror of the dove/ Pinions beating about the room
      Terror of all terrors that I bore
  5  The heavens in my womb

     A threefold terror — ~~the great star's dying~~   that star's fallen
          flare
     Entering through the hollow of an ear
     Some strange bird/ Those wings beating about the room
  4  The terror of all terrors that I bore
  5  The heavens in my womb

Yeats continued with a single draft of his second stanza, and multiple drafts of his third.

   ✕  I loved what everybody does or knows
   ✕  Toil and the sound of friendly shoes
     How beautiful are common sights and shows
     Voice face footfall that one knows
     ~~Carpenter bench~~   Chimney corner and garden walk
     That rocky cistern where we tread the clothes
 10  And gather all the talk

   ✕  He is all mine I bought him with my pains
   ✕  All mine, that my own milk sustains

   ✕  I call that mine
   ✕  All mine is He that my milk sustains

✕ I bore him [in] my bodily pains
✕ But my heart seems to stop

✕ What horror comes amid my body's pains
✕ Have [I] not bought that body with my pains
✕ What is that mouth that my milk stains
✕ ~~What~~   Suddenly my heart seems to stop

✕ May I not call that mine by body's pains
✕ Bought, or that my breast sustains
✕ I cry but my heart seems to stop
✕ And something shakes a chillness through my veins
✕ And the hair of my head stands up.

What could I more than buy him with my pains?
His mouth is mine that my milk stains?
What can have made my heart's blood stop
What can have struck the chill into my veins
What makes my hair stand up

Yeats wrote another version of "The Mother of God" on a detached sheet, and dated it. It is printed below:

[MS. 2]

## THE MOTHER OF GOD

### I

~~A three-fold~~   ~~Love that is~~   A three-fold terror — that star's
        fallen flare
Entering through the hollow of an ear
~~Wings that beat about~~   ~~Those wings beating~~   ~~These~~ strange
        wings beating in the room
Terror of all terrors that I ~~bear~~  bore
5 The heavens in my womb.

### II

✕ How beautifully a common ~~morning~~   evening goes
✕ How beautiful are common sights and ~~sounds~~   shows
How pleasantly the daylight comes and goes
✕ Voice, face footfall that one knows

Nothing there but what one knows
8 Chimney corner, garden walk
That rocky cistern where we tread the clothes
10 And gather all the talk

### III

✕ Have I not bought him with my pains
✕ What could I more than buy him with my pains?
✕ His mouth is mine that my milk stains
✕ But what has made my heart's blood [stop]?
✕ What can have struck the chill into my veins?
✕ What makes my hair stand up?

✕ Mine; my heart's blood seems to stop
✕ ~~Something has struck~~   And something strikes a chill into my
        ~~veins~~
✕ The hair of my head stand up.
✕ And makes my hair stand up.

Mine, mine my body purchased with its pains
A body that my milk sustains
Mine: my heart's blood seems to stop
Something has struck a chill into my bones
And made my hair stand up.

W. B. Y.   Sep 3   1931

Typescript 1 is an uncorrected carbon of a clean copy of the above. It seems to have been transcribed from the MS., for there are many blanks, and it is not very accurate. Yeats returned to his manuscript book and continued work on the poem in a series of drafts written in pencil. I have called these MS. 3 and MS. 4:

[MS. 3]

I

Threefold terror of love: a fallen flare
Etc. etc

        that I bore
Etc.

    I I

✕  How

✕  Pleasantly the morning goes

✕  Nothing there but what

✕  P

                    common daylight shows

    How pleasantly the daylight comes and goes

    Nothing but what one knows


    I I

✕  I had

 6  Had I not found content among the shows

 7  Every common woman knows

 8  Chimney corner, garden walk

 9  C̶i̶s̶  Or rocky cistern where we tread the clothes

10  And gather all the talk

✕  A̶l̶t̶h̶o̶u̶g̶h̶  Though my common

✕  But that I purchased with my body's pains

✕  That my mother's milk sustains

✕  The


    I I I

✕  My/ Mine, mine, my body purchased with its pains

✕  A body that my milk sustains

✕  B̶u̶t̶  Mine but what has made my heart's blood stop

✕  And what has struck the chill into my bones

✕  And made my hair stand up


    I I I

11  What is this flesh I purchased with my pains

12  This fallen star my milk sustains

13  This love that makes my heart's blood stop

14  Or strikes a sudden chill into my bones

15  And makes my hair stand up

    In the next draft Yeats made a clean copy of his poem, revising as
he went along; when he had finished the poem was nearly done.

[MS. 4]

## ~~THE ANNUNCIATION~~ MARY VIRGIN

### I

Threefold terror of love; a fallen flare
2 ~~Entering~~   Through the hollow of an ear;
3 ~~Those~~   Wings beating about the room;
4 The terror of all terrors that I bore
5 The heavens in my womb

### II

6 Had I not found content among the shows
7 Every common woman knows
8 Chimney corner, garden walk,
9 Or rocky cistern where we tread the clothes
10 And gather all the talk.

### III

11 What is this flesh I purchased with my pains
12 This fallen star my milk sustains
13 This love that makes my heart's blood stop
14 Or strikes a sudden chill into my bones
Or makes my hair stand up

In TS. 2, printed below, "The Mother of God" reaches its final
form. The change of "makes" to "bids" in the final line suggests that
TS. 2 may have been part of the copy for Macmillan's *Winding Stair*,
for this change was first printed there. It may, that is, be later than
the Cuala Press's *Words for Music*.

[TS. 2]

## THE MOTHER OF GOD

### I

1 The three-fold terror of love; a fallen flare
2 Through the hollow of an ear;
3 Wings beating about the room;
4 The terror of all terrors that I bore
5 The Heavens in my womb.

II

6  Had I not found content among the shows
7  Every common woman knows,
8  Chimney corner, garden walk,
9  Or rocky cistern where we tread the clothes
10  And gather all the talk.


III

11  What is this flesh I purchased with my pains,
12  This fallen star my milk sustains,
13  This love that makes my heart's blood stop
14  Or strikes a sudden chill into my bones
15  And ~~makes~~ bids my hair stand up?

One of the last entries in the manuscript book Yeats had used to write several versions of "The Mother of God" has to do with that poem. It was Yeats's habit when he thought of a correction for one of his finished poems to record the correction in whatever manuscript book he was using at the moment. These particular corrections were never introduced into the printed text.

> corrections in "Mother of God"
> Love's threefold terror — that star's fallen flare
> In the hollow etc.
>      and further down
> "That star" not "This star"
>      July 13, 1933

These drafts show that Yeats had the plan of "The Mother of God" fully worked out before he began to write. He had decided that the poem was to be a dramatic monologue; in the drafts as in the printed poem Mary is speaking, and in both she begins with the terrors of the annunciation, then goes on to contrast her peaceful past with her present state now that she has borne God. Once the drafts are underway, Yeats establishes his stanza pattern quickly, which combines the rhyme scheme aabab with lines using a varying number of stresses, 5, 4, 4, 5, 3.

In MS. 1 Yeats makes Mary's terror at the annunciation threefold from the outset; he then goes on to experiment with a series of lines all beginning with the word "terror" which state in varying ways the events that filled her with fear. One source of terror, a "voice out of the air," Yeats soon abandons, settling on the fallen star that strikes Mary through the ear, the presence of the Paraclete in the form of a dove, and her fear of impregnation by the divine. All of this comes very quickly, as do the rhyme sounds and even the rhyme words that Yeats will use in the finished poem. Two of these — room and ear — he finds in the very first draft, in reverse order; at his third essay he turns these around, and in his fourth shapes up his entire first stanza, getting line 5, adapted from the prose version of the poem, in final form. In his sixth draft, Yeats adds detail, and with it the poem takes on an immediacy it has lacked hitherto: "The shaft that struck me in the ear" becomes "Bursting through the hollow of an ear": "The terror of the dove in [the room]" becomes "Pinions beating about the room." Yeats then nearly completes his fourth line by changing "bear" to "bore." Mary speaks this poem after the birth of Christ, and because she does the rhyme "ear / bear" must be abandoned and the "a" rhymes in stanza 1 reduced to the slight consonance of the r-sounds. The stanza is nearly finished in Yeats's seventh draft. Yeats almost achieves his eventual first line when he writes "A threefold terror — that star's fallen flare"; he finishes line 4. As was usually true with Yeats, the thought is more directly, more obviously expressed in this version than in the printed poem. Yeats names the star, for instance; eventually he will merely allude to it. Apparently he became too allusive, for he added a note about the star when he reprinted the poem in *The Winding Stair*.

Yeats quickly roughs in his second stanza before going on to the third. In the drafts of lines 6 and 7 he clearly isn't trying very hard; whatever is amiss can be set right after the more interesting problems posed by stanza 3 are solved. Even in this hasty draft he does establish four rhyme words (knows, walk, clothes, talk) and completes line 10.

Yeats begins the drafts of stanza 3 in declarative statement; then in the third draft he changes to interrogative statement. These are partial drafts. In the fourth draft Yeats attempts his entire stanza, establishing the general movement of his thought and placing four rhyme words. In this draft lines 11 and 12 are interrogative, lines 13–15 declarative. In the fifth draft Yeats uses questions throughout, in fact there is excessive insistence on the questioning in the "what" repeated four times as the first word in lines 11, 13, 14, and 15.

At the end of these first drafts "The Mother of God" would have read as follows had Yeats assembled a clean copy:

A threefold terror—that star's fallen flare
Entering through the hollow of an ear
Those wings beating about the room
4 The terror of all terrors that I bore
5 The heavens in my womb

How beautiful are common sights and shows
Voice face footfall that one knows
Chimney corner and garden walk
That rocky cistern where we tread the clothes
10 And gather all the talk

What could I more than buy him with my pains?
His mouth is mine that my milk stains?
What can have made my heart's blood stop
What can have struck the chill into my veins
What makes my hair stand up

Yeats has made good progress, but there are many rough spots in the diction, and the draft notably lacks the metrical subtlety of Yeats's later poetry where every possible variation of a basic iambic pattern can usually be found. Manuscript 2 develops directly from MS. 1, indeed Yeats copies out most of the readings found there before experimenting with others. In stanza 1 he makes slight alterations in lines 3 and 4: line 3 becomes "Strange wings beating in the room"; in line 4 the initial "The" is dropped. In the draft of stanza 2 Yeats explores new detail to express Mary's content with her earlier lot: the beauty of the evening, the pleasantness of daylight — beautiful and pleasant because they are known. Manuscript 2 ends with two complete and one partial draft of stanza 3. At the close of MS. 1 this stanza had been a series of questions. In MS. 2 Yeats begins in the interrogative, then in the partial and complete drafts that follow shifts to the declarative. In the last version found here Mary insists that Christ is her child by a three-fold repetition of "Mine," and she insists he is a mortal child "my body purchased with its pains/ A body that my milk sustains." She then goes on to admit her fear of the supernatural. Yeats has shifted from present to past tense.

Manuscripts 3 and 4 are exercises in refinement. In stanza 1 the revision of the first line is particularly incisive. The phrase "terror of love" which Yeats here invents is the perfect beginning of the poem. Not only does it state the theme and establish the mood of the poem, it also states a paradox; introduces, that is, an ideational element into Mary's monologue which has the important effect of slightly altering her role. The participant is in the process of becoming participant-observer. By the time these revisions are finished this more complex conception of Mary's role has been established. In line 4 Yeats confirms an earlier decision to use the past tense "I bore"; he decides, that is, to abandon rhyme in favor of consonance. This will affect the revision of line 14.

Yeats had left stanza II in a very rough state, especially lines 6 and 7. Now he explores briefly various details from MS. 2, then writes off the stanza in its finished form. I feel that the decision that led so quickly to a final draft was the decision to use "shows" (line 6) as a noun instead of as a verb. The rest of the changes grow out of that one.

There are three drafts of the last stanza, the first partial, the second and third complete. In the first the principal change is the use of "purchase" in place of "buy": one does not "buy" the child one bears, though one may properly "purchase" him, that is acquire him by effort. In the second draft Yeats experiments again with combining declarative statement and question. In the fourth draft in MS. 1 Yeats had made lines 11 and 12 a question, then gone on to declaration; in MS. 2 he had used declarative statements throughout his latest version; now lines 11 and 12 declare while lines 13–15 question. In MS. 1 Yeats had used the present tense; he had shifted to the past tense in MS. 2; this he keeps in MS. 3 for his first and second drafts. The revision of line 14 shows Yeats's solution of a technical problem. Yeats has reduced the "a" rhyme in stanza 1 at line 4 to a slight consonance — flare, ear, bore — while in stanza 2 line 9 rhymes exactly with lines 6 and 7 — shows, knows, clothes. When Yeats changes "chill in my veins" to "chill in my bones" the a rhymes in stanza 3 conform with the pattern of stanza 1. In the third draft Yeats achieves the lines he first printed. He shifts back to the present tense, bringing Mary out of her recollective mood into the terror and immediacy of the passing moment, and he again, as in the fifth draft in MS. 1 and the first draft in MS. 2, makes the entire stanza a series of questions. This rush of questions on the nature of God, now phrased with ultimate refinement, completes the process of making Mary both participant in and observer of the birth of Christ. The poem gains power and interest as Mary's role acquires an aspect in which both poet and reader can participate. Finally, Yeats changes line 12 by writing "The fallen star my milk sustains" in place of "A body that my milk sustains." This echo of line 1 ties the poem together into a completely articulated unit; it should have made unnecessary the explanation Yeats wrote for *The Winding Stair*.

Yeats now copied his poem out clean in MS. 4. He tried two titles, "The Annunciation" and then "Mary Virgin," neither of which he kept. He eventually returned to the fine title found at the head of MS. 2. Yeats made slight improvements in stanza 1; for stanzas 2 and 3 he merely copied versions he had already completed. The second line of stanza 1 had read "Entering through the hollow of an ear"; Yeats deleted "entering," no doubt to make his line conform with the second lines of his succeeding stanzas, each of which has four stresses. Yeats first wrote "Those wings beating about the room," derived from MS. 1; he now deleted "those" to make his third line begin with an unmistakably strong accent after the long pause marked by the semicolon at the end of line 2. During the process of this draft he gave more attention to his pointing than hitherto, but he has by no means finished punctuating his poem.

Yeats had now essentially the version of the poem he would shortly print. At some later time Yeats softened the beginning of his poem by writing "The threefold terror of love." Then, after the poem had appeared in the Cuala Press's *Words for Music Perhaps*, Yeats made one more textual change, that recorded in TS. 2. The last line had read "And makes my hair stand up"; Yeats raises the intensity of his drama to the ultimate pitch possible when he changes this to read "And bids my hair stand up."

Yeats very early came to believe that an age begins with the birth of its god. Altogether he wrote four poems which concern the actual or imagined beginnings of new ages: "The Secret Rose" 1896, "The Second Coming" 1919, "Leda and the Swan" 1923, and "The Mother of God" 1931. "The Secret Rose" is apocalyptic; it foresees the death of an old order and the birth of a new and better, a new order presided over by the tutelary symbol of the Rose. "The Second Coming" records the death of the hopes Yeats had expressed in "The Secret Rose": a new age has indeed dawned, but its deity is not the Rose, but rather the stony, enigmatic sphinx. Then while at work on A *Vision* Yeats wrote magnificently of the incarnation which began the Classical age in "Leda and the Swan." Finally, in the poem we have been studying, he wrote of the beginning of the Christian era.

Yeats created one of his finest and most objective personae in "The Mother of God," and because he did he is able to realize and express attitudes toward the birth of Christ which he did not share. Yeats was no admirer of Mary, and he did not consider Christianity a satisfactory religion. He has told us so in many places, as in the second of the "Supernatural Songs" where Ribh denounced Patrick explicitly for maintaining that the Eternal begat Christ on a virgin. Yeats expressed his attitude even more sharply in a phrase near the end of entry XXXI of *Pages from a Diary Written in Nineteen Hundred and Thirty* (1944). In manuscript the passage reads:

Yet I must bear in mind that an antithetical revelation will be less miraculous (in the sense of signs and wonders) more psychological than a primary which is from beyond man and mothered by the void (Mary Virgin).

It is Yeats's sense of Mary, the persona who speaks the poem, that enables him here to control material that we would not expect him to be attracted to; it is precisely this persona that makes the material useable. The event is instructive. It was argued above that the relative weakness of much of Yeats's early verse comes from the weakness of his personae, the narrative voices invented for those poems, and that Yeats's strong style developed only after he had posited, so to speak, first person personae who are in some sense always Yeats, direct or antithetical. In the good poems this is a Yeats completely contained in his phantasmagoria, which is to say that the observation or biographical event which is often the starting point of a poem has been made "intended, complete" when the poem is done. One can go even further and claim with some confidence that with all of Yeats's male personae — Ribh, Old Tom, Malachi Stilt-Jack, John Kinsella — the principal thing involved is the degree of disguise that the mask chosen provides.

I do not think this is true of Yeats's women personae except in the literal sense that Yeats created all of them: they are by no means always Yeats and with them from very early on Yeats was able to achieve great objectivity, indeed an increasing objectivity which perhaps culminates in "The Mother of God." From Moll Magee on all the way to Crazy Jane these women are a great crew, and when Yeats uses them to speak his poems the problem of controlling his own accidence seems seldom to arise. "A Woman Young and Old" is a case in point: This sequence gave Yeats a great deal of trouble and was underway for many years (Yeats once thought it would be ready for inclusion in *The Tower*), but when it was done it was done (intended, complete) to a greater degree than "A Man Young and Old" where biographical accidence is not always controlled.

I can offer only probable explanations for this; no doubt Yeats himself might have found it difficult to explain. Doesn't the creative act, the imagined stance have built into it a necessary degree of objectivity when a writer who is a man undertakes to speak as a woman? Surely Molly is less Joyce than either Stephen or Bloom, though neither Stephen nor Bloom are Joyce involved in accidence, which is not to say that Molly is a greater creation, and surely the mother who speaks "Lullaby" and Mary who speaks "The Mother of God" are less Yeats than Ribh and John Kinsella not to speak of the "I" of "Byzantium." Yeats is more present in "Lullaby" than in "The Mother of God" for it seems unlikely that any actual mother ever thought of comparing the sleep of her child who has finished nursing with the sleep that overcame the world's great mythic lovers following consummation. The idea is daring, typical of Yeats, and it makes his "Lullaby" unique in the language. Such material would be immediately attractive, whereas much of the material in "The Mother of God" would not be (although Yeats might have seen in the woman with God in her belly a dark conceit of the artist, and he wrote in "A Packet for Ezra Pound" — first printed in 1929, this became part of A *Vision* in 1937 — of his own terror in the presence of the supernatural, a terror which he had just presented in other terms in *The Resurrection*).

Whatever the reason, none of Yeats's customary irritation with the nullity of virginity creeps into "The Mother of God." Rather he first imagines and then beautifully states how a simple peasant woman might have felt when caught up in these ponderous events; as she concludes her soliloquy she is no longer a simple peasant, but truly the Mother of God.

*ii*

## "Vacillation," Section VIII

YEATS BEGAN "VACILLATION" at Coole in November 1931, and worked on it for several months. Some twenty-four of the very large pages of the manuscript book used while composing "The Mother of God" are filled with drafts of "Vacillation." The entire process of Yeats's creation of this splendid poem can be followed in the sheets of the manuscript book, but this was so complex that to do so would require a long monograph. Richard Ellmann has reproduced and analysed many of the drafts of section VII; I have chosen section VIII for study. Here is Yeats's first draft:

> My teacher is not Von Hugel ~~though I scarce less than he~~
>       although both he and I
> Accept the miracles of the saints, honour their sanctity
> X Seventy or eighty years ago St. Teresa's tomb
> That St. Teresa's body lies undecayed in the tomb
> ~~Moistened by strange~~ Bathed in miraculous oil, or that sweet
>       odours from it come
> X Has once
> X Does not astonish me
> X Is not more
> X Is not more strange than sights that I have seen
> X Cannot ~~more~~ astonish more
> Does not seem more strange than sights that I have seen —
>       Perchance
> X Those learned hands
> X Hands that prepared the Pharaoh's
> X Learned fingers that prepared the Pharaoh's sacred mummy once
> X Now mummify the saints
> The hands that ~~made ready~~ readied for the tomb, the Pharaoh's
>       sacred mummies once
> Now mummify the saints
> X Bathed in miraculous oil or that
> X Bathed in sweet
> That it exudes miraculous ~~fragrant~~ sweet oil, or that perchance/
>       those hands

~~The hands~~ ~~that~~ ~~readied~~ ~~for~~ ~~the~~ ~~tomb~~   Turned into a mummy the
      Pharaohs' mummies once
Now mummify the saints. I ~~hold~~   think ~~things~~   well worthy of
      belief.
And that the examples of their lives ~~can~~   might bring ~~the~~   my
      heart relief
And set me on the heavenly [?]; and yet declare that I
✕ And yet I sw
✕ Yet swear to god that I
✕ And sanctify the soul, and yet I swear to god that I
✕ With fierce unchristened heart shall live in Homer's company
✕ ~~And~~ ~~set~~ ~~the~~ ~~soul~~ ~~by~~ ~~heaven's~~ ~~path~~   my ~~feet~~ ~~in~~ ~~heaven's~~ ~~way~~   the
      ~~feet~~ ~~in~~ ~~heaven's~~ ~~way~~   And set me upon heaven's way,
      and yet I swear that I
✕ With fierce unchristened heart ~~must~~   shall live in Homer's
      company
Must keep heart unchristened and walk in Homer's way
✕ And cast my soul upon the wind
✕ And turn my breast
✕ And lean my breast upon ~~the~~   that bitter wind
✕ Turn my breast toward the wind, my feet upon the way
✕ And
✕ Turn only what the fierce heart sang
The ~~lion's~~ ~~jaw~~ ~~the~~ ~~honey~~ ~~comb~~   Honey and the fierce animal, what
      was it Scripture said
~~I~~ ~~renounce~~   So   I therefore shut Von Hugel but with blessing
      on his head
And set my feet on heaven's path and yet declare that I
Must keep my heart unchristened, like Homer live [and] die
Honey and
The lion and the honey comb what was it

The second draft went as follows:

✕ Von Hugel's ~~is~~   not my teacher and yet both he and I
Must we part Von Hugel, though alike in this that we
Accept the miracles of the saints, honour their sanctity.
80 The body of St Teresa lies undecayed in ~~the~~ tomb;
   ~~Exudes~~ ~~miraculous~~ ~~oil~~   ~~Miraculous~~ ~~oil~~ ~~exudes~~ ~~from~~ ~~it~~   Bathed in
      some miraculous oil; sweet odours from it come,

X ~~The kings rule and the saints rule~~ Kings have ruled and saints
    may rule; those ghostly hands perchance
X That altered Pharaoh's body to a sacred mummy once
X Have mummified Theresa. Might find relief
X In study of lives like hers, belief like her belief
X And all such things delight me, and yet I swear that I
X Must keep my heart unchristened, like Homer live and die.
88X The lion and the honey comb what has scripture said:
  X I have shut Von Hugel though with blessings on his head.
82 Healing from its lettered slab; ~~those phantom hands~~ ~~the ghosts~~
    ~~of those~~ ~~those very hands~~ those selfsame hands per-
    chance
   That altered Pharaoh's body to a sacred mummy once
   Now mummify the saints; but I though heart might find relief
   If I became/ Had/ Did I become a Christian man, or ~~chose~~
    ~~choose~~ ~~chose~~ choose for my belief
86 What seems most welcome in the tomb, ~~play a different part~~ ~~play~~
    ~~out my chosen part~~ play a predestined part.
   Make Homer my example and his unchristened heart
88 The lion and the honeycomb what has scripture said:
  X ~~I have~~ There, I have shut Von Hugel though with blessings on
    his head.
   So get you gone Von Hugel though with blessings on that head.

Here is the third draft:

78 Must we part Von Hugel, though ~~alike in this that~~ much alike
    for we
79 Accept the miracles of the saints and honour sanctity.
80 The body of St. Teresa lies undecayed in tomb
81 Bathed in miraculous oil, sweet odours from it come
82 Healing from its lettered slab. Those self same hands perchance
  X That ~~altered~~ scooped out Pharaoh's body to a sacred mummy
    once
  X Now mummify the saints.
83 Eternalised the body of a modern saint that once
   Had scooped out Pharaoh's mummy. But I, though heart might
    find relief
85 Did I become a Christian man and choose for my belief
86 What seems most welcome in the tomb, play a predestined part

> Make Homer my example and his unchristened heart
> 88 The lion and the honey comb what has scripture said
> 89 So get you gone Von Hugel though with blessings on your head

Before Yeats began to write section VIII of "Vacillation," he had the plan of the poem clearly in mind and had decided on his metrical pattern. The pattern he picked uses long seven- and eight-stress lines rhymed in couplets, a pattern which he used to great effect in his later years. A comparison of this poem with Book III of *Oisin*, likewise written in long lines, will show how far Yeats had travelled toward complete mastery of the means of his art in forty-five years of constant writing. In the 1889 version the end of *Oisin* went as follows:

> I will pray no more with the smooth stones: when life in my body
>          has ceased —
> For lonely to move 'mong the soft eyes of best ones a sad thing were —
> I will go to the house of the Fenians, be they in flames or at feast,
> To Fin, Caolte, and Conan, and Bran, Sgeolan, Lomair.

It seems hardly possible that one poet could have come all the way from this to "Vacillation," where Yeats uses such a variety of metrical patterns with such complete command that the poem is a kind of set piece, so to speak, of metrical virtuosity.

The objects and situations used in the poem have also been fully assembled. The opening and closing allusions to Von Hügel, the allusion to the miraculously preserved body of St. Teresa, the reference to the doctrine of multiple existences in the account of the embalmer, the rejection of Christianity in favor of Homer's Paganism, the allusion to Samson's riddle — all of these things are present in the first draft and in the order they will have in the finished poem. In short, a large part of the work of composition had been done before Yeats began to write; the drafts show his search for expression.

An examination of the first draft shows that ten of the twelve rhyme sounds are in place (all except those used in lines 86 and 87), and nine of the rhyme words finally used (two of these "belief/ relief" will be inverted). These drafts are another example of how tenaciously Yeats clung to his rhyme words once he had established them. In draft 1 Yeats does not finish any of his lines, though line 88 is nearly finished: "The lion and the honey comb, what was it Scripture said."

One of the most skillful things in the finished poem is Yeats's management of person and number. There he begins with "we" — that is, himself and Von Hügel ("Must we part, Von Hugel"). The parting predicted in the opening question takes place in lines 84–86 when Yeats writes "I . . . play a predestined part," shifts, that is, from the first person plural to the first person singular. He then goes on to contrast his faith and Von Hügel's and to bid Von Hügel farewell. Yeats invented this artful management slowly. The first draft is in the first person singular throughout. While working on his second draft Yeats discovered the arrangement he was to keep, wherein the syntax itself reflects the parting that is the subject of the poem.

The use of the first person singular throughout the first draft involved Yeats in another difficulty which, again, he avoided in the second draft. The use of "I" brought too much of Yeats's personal accidence into the poem, brought, for instance, a reference to Yeats's own experience of the supernatural in the first draft of lines 80–82:

> That St. Teresa's body lies undecayed in the tomb
> Bathed in miraculous oil, or that sweet odours from it come
> Does not seem more strange than sights that I have seen —

Yeats revised this to read

> The body of St. Teresa lies undecayed in tomb
> Bathed in some miraculous oil; sweet odours from it come
> Healing from its lettered slab.

All accidence is gone from this revised version.

Yeats near the end of this first draft writes in three different ways of his own heart as unchristened:

> I swear to god that I
> With fierce unchristened heart shall live in Homer's company
> Must keep heart unchristened and walk in Homer's way
> Must keep my heart unchristened, like Homer live [and] die

In the second draft "unchristened heart" is transferred to Homer with happy results. Yeats bids loving farewell to Christianity in section VIII of "Vacillation"; poses and answers the question with whom shall the poet walk, Von Hügel or Homer? A drama of spiritual vacillation is unfolding, but when Yeats writes of his own "fierce unchristened heart" he has unfolded it before the climax. Since the phrase "unchristened heart" is too good to lose, Yeats transfers it appropriately to Homer, one of Dante's virtuous Heathen and Yeats's own forebear in the eternal world of art. This change like the others noted shows Yeats's highly skilled management of the "I-persona" here and throughout his later poetry.

This first draft is a remarkable achievement. Perhaps the happiest stroke in the finished poem is Yeats's allusion to Samson's riddle; it would have spoiled the poem to quote "Out of the strong cometh forth sweetness." Yeats has so arranged things that the reader supplies this essential thought and is charmed by its ironic aptness to the situation of the unchristened artist. Yeats took this allusive approach even in his first draft. The cancellations make an interesting study. Most of the cancelled lines were dropped because Yeats immediately found better expression, but some of them again reflect his artful management of the "I-persona." This is especially apparent in the cancellation of such a line as, "And lean my breast upon that bitter wind."

In the second draft Yeats established all his rhyme words in final position, and finished four lines (80, 82, 86, 88). The best thing that happened in this second draft, aside from the shift from the first person singular already described, was Yeats's decision to make his poem an imagined conversation with Von Hügel rather than a mere consultation of Von Hügel's book. This more dramatic approach seems to have occurred to Yeats at the outset, where he cancels the first line adapted from draft 1 and writes, "Must we part Von Hugel, though alike in this that we." During the course of his work on this draft Yeats also made two adjustments noted above, that is he dropped the reference to his own experiences of the supernatural and transferred "unchristened" to Homer. He also accomplished some miraculous improvements in meter and wording. His revision of line 80 illustrates improved meter:

> The body of St. Teresa lies undecayed in the tomb —
> The body of St. Teresa lies undecayed in tomb.

It is hard to explain why the omission of "the" does so much for this line. Part of the improvement comes from the excision of the soft anapest. But part of the greatness of Yeats's later poetry comes from his paring away of everything that can be pared away, revealing by that paring the stark, inevitable outline. This is an example of such paring. Yeats greatly improved his diction as well as his sound and rhythm when he changed "play a different part" to "play a predestined part." In a religious discussion no word could be more highly charged than "predestined." Here some of the charge comes from the ironic fact that Yeats plays a predestined part in rejecting the very Christianity where doctrines of predestiny were once avidly discussed.

In the third and final draft Yeats finished ten of his twelve lines and nearly completed his work on the other two (84, 87). The most important change was the revision of lines 83–84. In the second draft these had read

> That altered Pharaoh's body to a sacred mummy once
> Now mummify the saints.

Yeats achieved his far more vivid lines in draft 3, on a second attempt.

> X That ~~altered~~ scooped out Pharaoh's body to a sacred mummy
>  once
> X Now mummify the saints.
> Eternalised the body of a modern saint that once
> Had scooped out Pharaoh's mummy.

Here it is not too much to say that in the contrast between "eternalised . . . saint" and "scooped out" Yeats achieves the maximum tension possible among the realms of discourse.

Two things are finally striking about this run of drafts. The first is the extent of the improvement Yeats achieves within a single draft. This is characteristic of his late prose as well as his late verse. The second is the increased freedom of statement regarding religious belief. In 1932, when he finished the eighth section of "Vacillation," Yeats was taking full advantage of retirement from public life.

### iii

## "Ribh considers Christian Love insufficient"

YEATS WROTE THIS REMARKABLE POEM along with most of the other "Supernatural Songs" in a bound manuscript book which he began to use in 1934. There are no dates in the drafts of the poem, but it is based on an experience which occurred in October 1933, in the trance-speaking of Mrs. Yeats. Yeats recorded the experience on October 17:

Oct. 17
George three nights ago lit incense — I did not ask why nor perhaps did

she know. Presently she went into trance and Dionastes came, giving sign. He insisted on being questioned. I asked about fifteenth multiple influx. He said "Hate God." We must hate all ideas concerning God that we possess, that, if we did not, absorption in God would be impossible. . . . Later on George went two or three times into momentary trance and always to repeat "hatred, hatred" or "hatred of God." I was, the voice once said, "to think about hatred."

What seems to me the growing hatred among men has long been a problem with me. [Transcribed from the MS.]

The drafts of "Ribh considers Christian Love insufficient" occur in the manuscript book between the drafts of "The Four Ages of Man" and "He and She"; Yeats sent drafts of these to Olivia Shakespear in letters written in August 1934. I feel reasonably certain that the poem was written, at least finished, at about that time. All the drafts of "Supernatural Songs" are extremely difficult to decipher; Yeats did not form the ends of his words, and his cancellations are unusually heavy. Yeats, then, wrote approximately as follows:

### [Draft 1]

&times; Hatred I seek
&times; Love is of God and comes unsought
   I c

   I cannot study love that is of God
3&times; I ~~hatred~~   study hatred with great diligence

&times; I can stu
&times; I do not seek for love love comes unsought

   I do not seek for love nor study it
   It comes unsought and passes human wit
&times; Because it comes from God
   I seek to study with great diligence
&times; Hatred for that is in my own control
   Those passions that I know and may control

[Parts of the next three lines are obscured by a blot]

&times; The only thing that [is] in my control
   ~~Is hatred that~~   Those [?] hatred that are purges of the soul
&times; Hatred; but in purging [?] of the soul

✕ [undeciphered line]
✕ Must leave it nothing but bare mind and sense
~~That leaves~~   me I would have nothing there but mind and sense

[From the side of the page]

    Hatreds that are a besom to the soul
    And leave it nothing but bare mind and sense [1]

 7 Why do I hate man woman or event
    Hatred delivered from the false lips lent
    By terror shows that they are alien [?]
    ~~When native to my soul~~   ~~Which native to the soul~~   Dare dark
        distress, age shows at last
✕ What things are native to my soul at last
    How that shall walk when all such things are past
    ~~Or how it~~   ~~How that has~~   Or how it walked before such things
        began

    There on a darker scene I must learn
    From all my thoughts of God in loathing turn
✕ All thoughts of God
15 From every thought of God mankind has had
    ~~The~~   Such thoughts are garments and the soul's a bride
    That cannot in such trash and tinsel hide
✕ By hating God it
    By hating Him it creeps more near to God

    [two cancelled lines undeciphered]
    Thereon must I through darker study learn
    I must leave the scene and in hatred learn
    ~~The core of hatred and in~~   To touch the core and in my hatred
        turn
15 From every thought of God mankind has had
    Thoughts are but garments, and the soul's a bride
    And cannot in such trash and tinsel hide
✕ By hating God it creeps more near to God
    ~~In hatred of God~~   By hating God it creeps more near to God

    In that last dark the soul cannot endure
20 A bodily or mental furniture
    But just as he with his own hands shall give

✕ How look
✕ How can
   What can she know unless he bid her know
✕ How look above her till he makes the show
✕ How live till in her
✕ How live till he in all her blood shall live
   Where can she look until he makes the show
24 How can she live till in her blood he live.

## [Draft 2]
## RIBH'S SECOND POEM AGAINST PATRICK

1 Why should I seek for love or study it
2 It is of God and passes human wit;
✕ I seek to study with all diligence
3 I study hatred with great diligence
4 For that's a passion in my own control
5 A sort of besom that can clear the soul
   Of everything that is not mind and sense.

7 Why do I hate man woman or event?
✕ Hatred delivered from the false light lent
✕ By terror shows what things are alien
8✕ That is a light my jealous soul has sent
✕ A light of terror deception free; it can
✕ Show dirt dust decay, show at last

7✕ Why do I hate man woman or event
✕ Hatred of man, thought, woman or event!
7 Why do I hate man woman or event?
8 That is a light my jealous soul has sent;
9 From terror and deception freed it can
   Show dirt, dust decay, show at last
   How soul shall walk when all such things are past
   Or how it̶ soul walked before such things began
✕ Then must I through deeper study learn
✕ To touch the centre and in hatred turn
✕ The apple's core and in my hatred turn
13 Then my delivered soul herself shall learn
14 A d̶e̶e̶p̶e̶r̶ darker knowledge and in hatred turn

15× From every thought of God ~~mankind has had~~ —
×                        my soul has had
15×                        mankind has had
 15 From every thought of God mankind has had
 — Thoughts are but garments and the soul's a bride
 17 That cannot in that trash and tinsel hide
     ~~In hatred of~~  ~~Through hating~~ In hating God she creeps more
               near to God
 19 At stroke of midnight soul ~~shall not~~  cannot endure
 20 A bodily or mental furniture
 × But such as he has given or shall give
 × What can she take until her master gives
     What ~~can~~  shall she take until ~~his hand can~~ [her] master give
 × But what his hand has given, ~~or shall give~~  what it gives.
 22 Where can she look until he ~~makes~~  make the show?
     What can she know until he ~~bid~~  bids her know?
 24 How can she live till in her blood he ~~lives~~  live?

"Ribh considers Christian Love insufficient" was nearly finished in this second draft, and Yeats made unusual progress toward his finished poem in the first. This raises the question whether these were all the drafts he made. I cannot answer with certainty, but think it possible that the poem was accomplished in these two drafts. Yeats's statement here is unusually clear and direct; he uses very few images until he develops the extended metaphor at the end, where the soul after death is seen to approach God as the bride approaches the bridal bed and the waiting bridegroom. When Yeats's later poetry is difficult, it is often because he is saying something he has said before, because he is stating, say, the doctrine of Unity of Being yet once more. Then he must find some new and often enigmatic way of speaking. Here the thought is at once fresh, striking, and intrinsically poetic. If my dating is correct and some ten months separated the eruption of these thoughts in Mrs. Yeats's trance and the writing of the poem, then Yeats had surely thought long and deeply before he began to write. This too would help to explain the speed and assurance with which he worked. I would like, in short, to suppose that the drafts of "Ribh considers Christian Love insufficient" show that sometimes Yeats was able largely to arrange a poem in his head before taking to pen and ink.

If there is anything to the case stated above, if there were no earlier drafts of the poem, then draft 1 is a remarkable accomplishment. The thought develops through the four stanzas as it will develop in the finished poem; Yeats finds many of the words and images he will retain. In the drafts of stanza 1, he makes three false starts, then writes a draft of the whole stanza during the course of which he puts all of his eventual rhyme words in place. The ironically incongruous metaphor wherein hatred becomes a broom that will sweep accumulated trash out of the soul, an idea which Yeats develops in stanza 2 of this draft, is invented after Yeats explores in two draft lines the possibility of making hatred a purge. Only line 3 is finished (Yeats has cancelled it), but the stanza pattern is set, the theme of the poem stated, the line ends established.

Yeats goes on to a single draft of stanza 2. He begins by writing down line 7 as it will appear in the finished poem. He continues with what seems to me a recollection of Dionastes' voice speaking through Mrs. Yeats's trance: "Hatred delivered from the false lips lent/ By terror." In the "Introduction" to A *Vision* Yeats speaks of the terror that often accompanied these inexplicable experiences. The old age theme erupts momentarily. All in all there is too much accidence here, too much that is directly personal. We will see Yeats retrench this accidence in draft 2. In draft 1 Yeats finishes line 7, and gets all of his rhyme sounds and four of his rhyme words into place.

There are two draft versions of stanza 3, neither of them cancelled — indeed in his later manuscripts Yeats cancelled far less systematically than in his earlier. In the drafts of line 13 the transition to "the other life" is stated with increasing force and clarity: "There on a darker scene I must learn/ Thereon must I through darker study learn/ I must leave the scene and in hatred learn." The second form of line 14 "To touch the core and in my hatred turn" will lead to an image in draft 2, one quickly abandoned. Yeats explores with great assurance the striking metaphor with which the stanza ends, wherein the soul once delivered from the body becomes a bride who creeps to God, the bridegroom, in the nakedness of the bridal surrender. By the end of these drafts Yeats has finished line 15 and all his rhyme words are in place.

Stanza 4 takes shape quickly. At the end of a single draft two lines are done (20 and 24), the rhyme words are all in place (Yeats will reverse lines 22 and 23 in the next draft), and Yeats is experimenting with the strong interrogatives (What, Where, How) which begin lines 21–24.

A clean copy of this first draft will help us compare it with the second:

> I do not seek for love nor study it
> It comes unsought and passes human wit
> I seek to study with great diligence
> Those passions that I know and may control
> Hatreds that are a besom to the soul
> And leave it nothing but bare mind and sense
>
> 7 Why do I hate man woman or event;
> Hatred delivered from the false lips lent
> By terror shows that they are alien
> Dare dark distress, age shows at last
> How that shall walk when all such things are past
> Or how it walked before such things began
>
> I must leave the scene and in hatred learn
> To touch the core and in my hatred turn
> 15 From every thought of God mankind has had
> Thoughts are but garments, and the soul's a bride
> And cannot in such trash and tinsel hide
> By hating God it creeps more near to God
>
> In that last dark the soul cannot endure
> 20 A bodily or mental furniture
> But just as he with his own hands shall give
> What can she know unless he bid her know
> Where can she look until he makes the show
> 24 How can she live till in her blood he live.

In draft 2 Yeats finishes his first stanza except for a single word (line 6 "mind and sense/ mind or sense"). Each of the finished lines is implicit in the lines of draft 1, but each is transmuted, as it were, to a higher level of expression. Yeats now begins with a question, strikingly phrased, then in lines 3–6 returns to the declarative pattern of draft 1. The improvement of line 2 is almost a miracle: "It comes unsought and passes human wit/ It is of God and passes human wit." In his cancelled third line Yeats reworks draft 1, then rewrites the line, lifting "hatred" out of line 5 to establish his love/ hate contrast at the very beginning of his poem. Yeats used the space opened in line 5 by the removal of "hatreds" to phrase his ironic comparison (hatred/ besom) more fully: "Hatreds that are a besom to the soul/ A sort of besom that can clear the soul."

Yeats left stanza 2 full of his accidence; now in two drafts he cuts this back severely. In the first draft of line 8 he alludes less directly to the supernatural source of his meditation on hatred, then he omits it entirely:

Hatred delivered from the false light lent/
That is a light my jealous soul has sent.

In the drafts of line 10 Yeats tries naming those things — dirt, dust, decay — that the besom hatred can sweep out of the soul. The draft line is metrically awkward and needs rewriting, yet the image is sharper than the "Discover impurities" of the finished poem, and it once tied stanza 2 strongly to stanza 1. (The image also anticipates the rag-and-bone shop of "The Circus Animals' Desertion.") The new forms of lines 11–12 show how much clarity and emphasis can be gained by replacing pronouns by nouns. In draft 1 "that" and "it" are used to refer back to the "soul" in line 5; Yeats now replaces them with "soul." Lines 7–9 are done, line 10 will be revised; lines 11–12 are nearly done.

In the drafts of stanza 3 Yeats first tries a more allusive statement of the transition from life to death; he also momentarily develops "core" into an image — he is going to learn the very core of the apple of knowledge of good and evil. He cancels this and replaces it with the direct statement of the finished poem:

I must leave the scene and in hatred learn
To touch the core and in my hatred turn [Draft 1]

Then must I through deeper study learn
To touch the centre and in hatred turn
The apple's core and in my hatred turn

13 Then my delivered soul herself shall learn
14 A darker knowledge and in hatred turn.

The rest of the stanza is carried over from draft 1 with very little change. Line 18 as first printed was very close to this draft:

In hating God she creeps more near to God
In hating God she may creep close to God. [*Poetry*, December 1934]

Yeats introduced the present reading in *A Full Moon in March*. Lines 13–15 and 17 are done, lines 16 and 18 nearly done.

In revising stanza 4 Yeats replaced "In that last dark" by the more immediate "At stroke of midnight" in line 19. He copied out line 20, and then went on to clear up the rhetorical form of the four ponderous questions with which the poem ends. A cancelled version of line 21 is closer to the final form of the line than the version Yeats allowed to stand in this draft, "What can she take until her master gives." I think that Yeats reversed lines 22 and 23 to avoid beginning two successive lines with "what," at least "what, where, what, how" is to my ear far better than "what, what, where, how." When Yeats rewrote "What can she know unless he bid her know" to read "What can she know until he bids her know," he decided to risk the obstinate repetition "until, until, until, till" which accounts for a large part of the sheer rhetorical strength of lines 21–24. When Yeats finishes his draft, his final stanza is nearly done.

## iv
### "The Gyres"

I HAVE CHOSEN "The Gyres" to show Yeats at work on one of *New Poems* (1938) because its successive drafts are still to be found in the looseleaf manuscript cover where Yeats wrote them, I think in the order in which he composed.[2] In addition to the drafts of "The Gyres," this manuscript book contains other very late poems, a scrap of dialogue from *Purgatory*, the "Creed," already quoted, on which "Under Ben Bulben" is based, and a trial table of contents for *New Poems*. Yeats dated the final draft of "The Gyres" "April 9." He did not add the year. Mrs. Yeats has dated the poem 1937, and I agree with this dating, since the contents of the book make it certain that Yeats was using it in 1937 and 1938. The drafts of "The Gyres" which I transcribe are items 6, 8, and 10 in this manuscript book. Item 7 is the scrap of dialogue from *Purgatory*, item 9 the table of contents of *New Poems*.

Item 6 is a draft of what is now stanza 3 of "The Gyres." I believe that Yeats wrote this first, and that the whole poem grew out of the comforting idea with which the finished poem ends, that the gyre of history will bring around again those human types that he most admired, "the workman, noble and saint." I suggest that Yeats invented the first two stanzas to stage, so to speak, the thought of the third stanza with which he began.

[Item 6]

×　And even as these three to meet it all again
×　Search the country sides and find the three
×　But then the joy

×　When all is broken
　　Though all be broken, all may yet be whole
×　Rocky face [?], if [you] can find these three
×　If you

　　Old rocky face if you can find the three
　　That can perfect ~~the~~　a work ~~the~~　a life the soul,
×　Go seek among the ruined valleys
×　Somewhere between the polecat and the owl
×　~~Under~~　Go seek the cobwebs of ~~old~~　dead villages
×　Or else between the polecat and the owl
×　They may be hidden in old villages
　　Somewhere among the abandoned villages
　　Or skulking between the polecat and owl
　　Upon a mountain among storm tossed [?] trees
　　Say these all [word undeciphered] or say that we repeat
　　~~Bring in~~　But bring the craftsman the noble and the saint

[There is another page of jottings for this stanza which I cannot transcribe. Item 8 consists of working drafts of stanzas I and II. These pages have been cancelled entire.]

## WHAT MATTER

I

×　What matter — wrinkled rocky face look forth
×　What's thought too long can be no longer thought

[From the facing page.]

×　What's thought? What's thought? Old rocky face look forth
×　What's thought too long must be no longer thought

[At this point Yeats marked lines 1 and 2 "stet."]

    And blood's irrational streams must wet the earth
    Those/ The three perfections ~~have been~~   must be blotted out;
    ~~But~~   Or here's a metaphor that has more pith
7  Hector is dead and there's a light in Troy
8  We that look on but laugh in tragic joy

      I I

    What matter ~~if~~   that the topless glories drop
    Into the mire and blood and take ~~its~~   ~~their~~   the stain
✕  Or that those sweaty gangsters live on top
✕  Or that base gangsters ~~are~~   clamber on the top,
✕  A greater and more gracious time has gone
✕  For greater and more gracious times have gone

[The next five lines are from the facing page.]

✕  That all the sweaty gangsters ride on top;
✕  ~~A~~   For greater and more gracious ~~time has~~   times have gone
    What matter if the ~~gangster~~   base man is on top
    And blood and mire our ancient [?] glory stain
I I  What matter heave no sigh let no tear drop

[Back to original page.]

    I sighed for bust or boxes of make up
    ~~From~~   In ancient tombs and shall not sigh again
    What matter — out of the cavern comes a voice
✕  And that has but a single word rejoice
✕  And one sole word it cries rejoice.
    And all commandment's in that word 'rejoice.'

[Yeats then made three more drafts of his first stanza. He cancelled all
of them.]

## WHAT MATTER

    What's thought too long — old rocky face look forth
    What's thought too long can be no longer thought
✕  And blood's irrational streams must wet the earth
✕  Those lineaments must all be blotted out

✗  But here's an image of more pith and worth
   Beauty of beauty dies and worth of worth
   ~~All~~    Then the old lineaments are blotted out
   The/ And the irrational ~~stream of blood has wet~~   blood stream
         wets the earth
   For the great gyres have tumbled us about
7  Hector is dead and there's a light in Troy
8  We that look on but laugh in tragic joy

   ~~What matter, what matter~~   Old cavern man, old rocky face look
         forth
2  Things thought too long can be no longer thought
   And beauty dies of beauty, worth of worth
   ~~Then the old~~   The ancient lineaments are blotted out
✗  For the irrational blood stream wets the earth
✗  The irrational stream of blood was wetting earth
   The irrational blood stream wets the earth
✗  For the great gyres have tossed us all about
   The ancient/ A furious gyre has tumbled us about
7  Hector is dead and there's a light in Troy
8  We that look on but laugh in tragic joy

1  The gyres! The gyres — old Rocky face look forth
2  Things thought too long can be no longer thought
3  ~~And~~   For beauty dies of beauty, worth of worth
4  ~~The~~   And ancient lineaments are blotted out
   The irrational blood stream ~~has wet all~~   begins to wet the earth
   Empedocles has tumbled us about
7  Hector is dead and there's a light in Troy
8  We that look on but laugh in tragic joy


[Item 10 is a dated draft of the complete poem.]

      I

1  The gyres, the gyres — old rocky face look forth
2  Things thought too long can be no longer thought
3  For beauty dies of beauty, worth of worth
4  ~~All~~   And ancient lineaments are blotted out
5  Irrational streams of blood are staining earth
6  Empedocles has thrown ~~our~~   all things about

7 Hector is dead and there's a light in Troy
8 We that look on but laugh in tragic joy

II

X What matter if blind ~~Fate~~   fury rides ~~on~~   upon the top

[The next line from the facing page.]

What matter though numb nightmare ride on the top
X And blood and mire the [word undeciphered] glory stain

[The next two lines from the facing page.]

X And blood and mire ~~all the rivers~~   the broken buildings stain
10 And blood and mire the sensitive body stain
11 What matter heave no sigh let no tear drop
   ~~For~~   A greater and more gracious time has gone
   ~~I sighed for~~   For painted bust or  boxes of make up
14 ~~From~~   In ancient tombs I ~~shall not sigh~~   sighed but not again
15 What matter — out of ~~the~~   cavern comes a voice
X And all commandment's in the word rejoice
16 And all it knows is that one word rejoice

III

X Perfection of the work, the life the soul!
   Come lineaments of work, conduct and soul
   ~~Orders that to old~~   Those lovers that to rocky face are dear
   Those lovers of horses and of women shall
   Out of ~~the~~   some stark oblivion disinter
   Dark between the polecat and the owl
   Or from the ruined [?] marble sepulchre
   ~~Artist~~   Workman noble and saint and all ~~things~~   shall run
24 ~~On~~   ~~Round~~   On that unfashionable gyre again.
                  April 9

Yeats finished "The Gyres" in two typescripts. In TS. 1 stanzas 1
and 2 are exact copies of those stanzas in the dated MS. printed just
above. Stanza 3 is a later version than that found in the MS.; perhaps
it copies a manuscript which I have not seen. Yeats corrected stanza 3
of TS. 1, but not stanzas 1 and 2. Stanza 3 from TS. 1 is given first as
typed and then as corrected, and the same stanza as corrected in TS. 2:

[TS. 1, stanza 3, as typed]

> Come lineaments of work, conduct and soul
> From dark and bright that Rocky Face holds dear
> 19 Lovers of horses and of women shall
> The Saint, the Noble, Workman, disinter;
> Darkness between the pole cat and the owl
> Bright marble of a broken sepulchre
> Bridles upon the horses, women; all shall run
> Upon that old forgotten gyre again.

[TS. 1, stanza 3, as revised]

> 17 Conduct and work grow coarse and coarse the soul;
> From dark and bright that Rocky Face holds dear
> 19 Lovers of horses and of women shall
> The Saint, Noble, and Workman, disinter;
> Darkness between the pole cat and the owl
> Bright marble of a broken sepulchre;
> 23 The Workman, Noble and Saint; and all things run
> 24 On that ~~old~~ unfashionable gyre again

[TS. 2, stanza 3, with Yeats's manuscript revisions]

> 17 Conduct and work grow coarse and coarse the soul,
> 18 What matter! ~~Some~~ Those that ~~old~~ Rocky Face holds dear,
> 19 Lovers of horses and of women, shall
> 20 From marble of a broken sepulchre
> 21 Or dark betwixt the polecat and the owl,
> 22 Or any rich, dark nothing disinter
> 23 The workman, noble and saint, and all things run
> 24 On that unfashionable gyre again.

Item 6, the early draft of what became Yeats's third stanza, shows, I believe, how fragmentary, inchoate even, the beginnings of Yeats's poems often were even at the end of his career. There is one slight bit of external evidence for my belief that here indeed is the germ from which the poem grew, the fact that it once stood first in the manuscript book. Since Yeats was working in a looseleaf manuscript cover, and since even when working in a bound manuscript book he often moved both back and forward from the sheet on which he began to write, this fact should be weighted rather lightly. The internal evidence is stronger, however. The whole idea of the poem is stated in the draft lines

> Though all be broken, all may yet be whole
> Old rocky face if you can find the three
> That can perfect a work a life [a] soul

The draft goes on with Rocky Face (in Mrs. Yeats's annotated copy of *Last Poems* Rocky Face is glossed as "Delphic Oracle") searching for the craftsman, noble and saint amid the ruins of civilization so that he may establish them again. Furthermore there is one line in the draft of stanza 1 in item 8 that makes it almost certain that Yeats composed item 6 before he composed item 8: "The three perfections must be blotted out." These bits of evidence, taken together, have led me to believe that Yeats began "The Gyres" by imagining some happier day when the process of history would bring back "the craftsman the noble and the saint," that he began where he now ends.

Item 8 begins with working drafts of stanzas 1 and 2 under the title "What Matter"; it continues with three successive drafts of stanza 1 during the course of which Yeats finishes that stanza. In these drafts both the poetic form and the progression of images Yeats will use in the finished poem emerge. In this draft of stanza 1 and in the draft of stanza 2 that follows, Yeats is experimenting with a seven-line stanza with three rhymes. He has not certainly established the pattern of his "a" and "b" rhymes, but has decided to end the stanza with a couplet. The rhyme scheme of stanza 1 is ababacc, of stanza 2 abaabcc; if Yeats had allowed a cancelled line, "For greater and more gracious times have gone," to stand in the drafts of stanza 2 as the fourth line, he would have achieved his eventual ottava rima scheme, abababcc.

Yeats sets a title, then picks up the words of the title, "what matter," to begin his poem. He fills in his decasyllable line with "wrinkled rocky face look forth," where the "r," "c," and "f" sounds form a rather cacophonous pattern. Furthermore, though skin wrinkles, does rock? Yeats cancels this, then tries a daring repetition of "What's thought":

> What's thought? What's thought? Old rockyface look forth
> What's thought too long must be no longer thought.

Yeats cancels this, and marks the lines first written "stet"; he has, however, written a metrical equivalent of the first line of his finished poem and found in "old" the epithet he will retain for "rocky face." We will see Yeats invent his present third line in a later draft; now he uses an early form of line 5 as his third line, "And blood's irrational streams must wet the earth." He continues with the line commented on above, "The three perfections must be blotted out." Perhaps Yeats came to feel that this said too much, that he could achieve a more dramatic statement if he retained the three for his last stanza. Yeats's fifth line seems to take us inside the writing process, so to speak, "Or here's a metaphor that has more pith." Yeats then struck off without blotting a word the couplet with which the first stanza still ends.

The allusion to the burning of Troy at the end of his first stanza brought to mind Marlowe's description, so Yeats begins his second stanza "What matter that the topless glories drop/ Into the mire and blood and take the stain." The echo of Marlowe is followed here by an echo of Yeats's own "Byzantium." No doubt Yeats felt that this was too literary, for when he returned to these lines later in this same draft, he cut the echo of Marlowe. He did this while exploring the possibility of making the American gangster top dog in the age he so disliked. (We have all seen so many gangster movies that it is a relief when this folk myth disappears after several experiments.)

> Or that those sweaty gangsters live on top
> Or that base gangsters clamber on the top
> That all the sweaty gangsters ride on top
> What matter if the ~~gangster~~  base man is on top

While playing with the gangster, Yeats drafts three forms of what is now line 12; he cancels all of them, with the result that a seven-line stanza again emerges with a rhyme scheme slightly different from that of the first draft of stanza 1. Yeats continues by writing off his eleventh line in final form. Lines 13–16 fall into place quickly; Yeats will adjust their diction and meter, but their substance is set. Yeats's progress with his second stanza has been remarkable. He has established the progression of images he will retain while cutting out those he does not want, his rhyme words are all in place, he has drafted a line with a "b" rhyme which he will be able to use when he decides on ottava rima form, he has finished line 11.

The first of the three successive drafts of stanza 1 which follow is the crucial one. During the course of this draft Yeats establishes his eight-line stanza, he rearranges his images and adds to them. Yeats composes five lines which come directly from the preceding draft, making a significant change in his fourth draft line when "The three perfections must be blotted out" becomes "Then the old lineaments are blotted out." This says much the same thing in a more suggestive and allusive way, while reserving "the three" for the final stanza; it also uses one of Yeats's favorite words, derived from Blake, rather differently from the way he had used it in writing of Maud Gonne. And when Yeats says in effect that the ancient bodily forms have been blotted out, is he not already on his way to poems and prose works concerned with eugenic reform? He continues with a new form of the line he had invented to introduce his closing couplet, "But here's an image of more pith and worth." It must have been clear to Yeats from the first that he would eventually cancel this line; he does so now, but makes it serve his purposes, for out of it he evolves his third line, which here reads, "Beauty of beauty dies and worth of worth." He then re-words lines 4 and 5 before inserting the gyres in line 6, "For the great gyres have tumbled us about." Their absence up to this point from a poem about the gyres has been rather surprising. Yeats finishes the draft by copying out the couplet which closed the stanza in draft 1.

In the second of these drafts Yeats is still experimenting with his first line. He tries his key words "what matter," which stood at the beginning of stanzas 1 and 2 in an earlier draft, then replaces these by "Old cavern man." He finishes line 2, and gets rid of the inverted syntax in line 3 when he writes "and beauty dies of beauty, worth of worth." In line 4, "Then the old lineaments" becomes "The ancient lineaments"; in line 6, "great gyres have tumbled" becomes "great gyres have tossed" and then "A furious gyre has tumbled us about." Again, there is no change in the concluding couplet.

In the third draft Yeats nearly finishes his first stanza. He makes a final and crucial change in the progression of his images when he moves the gyre from line 6 up to line 1, and repeats it. He has not yet added the title, but that is implied, surely, in this change. His poem will begin with "the gyres" three times repeated. Both the rhetoric and meter of this line repeat a beginning which Yeats tried and abandoned in his earliest draft, where the title "What Matter" was followed by a first line beginning "What's thought? What's thought?" Yeats finishes lines 1–4, revises line 5, and then introduces Empedocles into the space vacated by the gyre, no doubt moved to do so both

because of the marvelous sound of the name and because he thought
of Empedocles as an exponent of the cyclic tradition.

Item 10, a dated draft of the whole poem, is typical. Yeats finishes
stanza 1; he makes good progress toward the final form of stanza 2;
he leaves stanza 3, with which he had begun, far from finished. Very
often in manuscript versions of Yeats's poems the various parts of a
single poem are in various states of finish. The first four lines of
stanza 1 had been finished in the preceding draft. Yeats copies these
out, then makes an important change in line 5 when he changes "The
irrational blood stream begins to wet the earth" to "Irrational streams
of blood are staining earth." The revision knocks out two syllables
from what had been an awkward thirteener, and the introduction of
"staining" provides a link with line 10 of stanza 2. The change in
line 6 — "Empedocles has tumbled us about/ Empedocles has thrown
all things about" — was made, I feel, to get rid of "us"; the change
helps the reader to move easily from the bloodstained present to the
statement in the final couplet that such violence is recurrent, hence
eternal.

The changes made in stanza 2 will be seen more clearly if we begin
by looking at a clean copy of the first draft, with its cancelled fourth
line put in place:

> What matter if the base man is on top
> And blood and mire our ancient glory stain
> What matter heave no sigh let no tear drop
> X For greater and more gracious times have gone
> I sighed for bust or boxes of make up
> In ancient tombs and shall not sigh again
> What matter — out of the cavern comes a voice
> And all commandment's in that word 'rejoice.'

In line 9 "Fate," "fury," and finally "numb nightmare" replace the
"base man"; "numb nightmare ride on the top" is a powerful, an
almost furious phrase, and the line is done except for the excision of
"the" from "on the top." In line 10 Yeats introduces an almost miraculous improvement when he replaces "our ancient glory" with "the
sensitive body"; the metaphor was weak because an abstraction like
"ancient glory" cannot really be stained. Yeats copies out his finished
eleventh line and then establishes and slightly changes line 12. In
recasting lines 13–14 Yeats introduces an inverted sentence; this is

contrary to his usual practice of putting inverted sentences into normal order while revising. I think Yeats made the change primarily to avoid the repetition of "sigh," though it also opened a place for the effective epithet "painted." I suppose that Yeats changed "bust" to "forms" before printing the poem because in Egyptian tombs opened in the 1920's the painted figures were forms. Line 15 is finished when Yeats strikes out "the." Yeats first copies out line 16 from the preceding draft, changing one word; then he recasts the whole line, perhaps because "commandment's" is an awkward elision.

In the draft of stanza 3 that was once item 6 in Yeats's manuscript book, Yeats directed Rocky Face to find the three "That can perfect a work a life [a] soul," either among the abandoned villages of an old culture or from the mountain where they are "skulking between the polecat and the owl." Find them where he might, Rocky Face was to "bring the craftsman the noble and the saint." This roughly expresses the thought of stanza 3 in the finished poem, toward the expression of which Yeats moved in a series of four consecutive drafts. During these drafts Yeats dropped some correlatives (villages, a mountain), he invented a series of new correlatives (broken sepulchre, rich dark nothing, unfashionable gyre), and he provided Rocky Face with agents (lovers of horses and of women) to disinter "the three."

He starts to do this in the draft found at the end of the manuscript dated April 9. First he writes and cancels a line that grows directly out of a line found in the earlier draft: "That can perfect a work a life [a] soul." This now becomes "Perfection of the work, the life the soul!" Since "the three" are notably absent from the two stanzas Yeats has completed, stanzas in which he has magnificently stated the historical and cultural situation which requires the return of "the three," the meaning of this new line is enigmatic. It is enigmatic because it looks too far forward. Not until we finish the stanza do we know that we can achieve the three perfections only if lovers dear to Rocky Face disinter the workman we admire for his work, the noble we admire for his life, and the saint we admire for his soul. Yeats expresses his meaning somewhat more clearly when he writes, "Come lineaments of work, conduct and soul." The repetition of "lineaments" takes us back to line 4: "And ancient lineaments are blotted out," and because it does serve as a useful link between the last stanza and the first. Since "lineaments" as used in this poem clearly means "bodily forms," Yeats is now saying "may the bodily forms associated with right work, right conduct, and right soul come again"; this prepares us for the action described in the remaining lines.

Yeats now largely invents lines 18–23 wherein the lovers dear to Rocky Face "shall disinter" the workman, noble, and saint from a "stark oblivion" foreshadowed by the "dead villages" of the earlier draft. Lines 21 and 22 particularize this stark oblivion. The earlier draft had ended by naming the three;[3] now Yeats names them in line 23, and invents in final form the last line which rounds out his poem by naming the new gyre which will replace the unsatisfactory gyre now operative. At the end of this draft Yeats has finished line 24 and set all his line ends, though in his final draft he will transpose "sepulchre" and "disinter."

Yeats completed stanza 3 in TS. 1 and 2. The three drafts to be discussed are particularly fascinating because in them Yeats reworks the stanza radically without altering any of his line ends. It is as though a terrific disturbance in the center of a pool took place without disturbing the waters on its circumference, or as if a painter completely rearranged the center of a picture while leaving its outer portion unchanged. This is a final proof of Yeats's extreme unwillingness to alter a form he had once set.

In the typed words of TS. 1 Yeats changes the order of his correlatives and slightly changes his meaning. In the dated manuscript Yeats had filled out his form by using "Those lovers" in lines 18 and 19:

> Those lovers that to rocky face are dear
> Those lovers of horses and of women shall;

He had also spread wide the main elements of his clause (lovers shall disinter workman noble and saint). Yeats gets rid of the tautology by slightly changing his detail:

> From dark and bright that Rocky Face holds dear
> Lovers of horses and of women shall . . .

He tightens his spread syntax by inclosing his direct objects ("The Saint, the Noble, Workman") between the two parts of the verb "shall disinter." His solution does not work: the brightness here introduced to contrast with the dark distorts Yeats's meaning; the transposition of "the three" from line 23 to line 20 leaves a gaping hole in line 23 which Yeats fills up anyhow by writing "Bridles upon the horses, women." While trying to fix lines 17–20 Yeats ruins lines

21–24, even in their detail, as when in line 24 he replaces "unfashionable gyre" with "old forgotten gyre."

Yeats accomplishes some of the necessary repairs in his revision of TS. 1. He begins these by inventing a new seventeenth line which still stands: "Conduct and work grow coarse and coarse the soul." This at once summarizes the situation described in stanzas 1 and 2, and points toward the need to disinter "the three" who will demonstrate right conduct, work, and soul. Yeats then tries the effect of naming the three both at line 20 and line 23, with very awkward results. His syntax no longer works, but he has somehow got the three back into his penultimate line where they need to be. A few more changes, the most important being the return to the text of the felicitous epithet "unfashionable," and lines 23 and 24 are done. Yeats has still to rework his syntax and further adjust lines 18, 20, 21, and 22.

In the revised TS. 2 Yeats solves all his remaining problems. He first writes a new and final eighteenth line which begins by repeating the phrase "what matter" for the fourth time. He drops the "dark and bright that Rocky Face holds dear" and fills out the line with "those that Rocky Face holds dear," a reworking of line 18 in the dated manuscript. He finishes lines 20–22 by spreading open still further the two parts of his verb "shall disinter" so that they now frame these lines. Within this frame Yeats rearranges his detail: he revises what had been line 22 to make his now finished twentieth line, and invents new matter for line 22, matter which further describes the enigmatic dark from which "the three" are to be disintered. Stanza 3 is done; the poem is done save for a little touching up of stanza 2.

V

## "The Circus Animals' Desertion"

YEATS WROTE the first complete draft of "The Circus Animals' Desertion" in London during November 1937. In this manuscript the first four stanzas are very like the poem we know, save that the key or theme word of the poem, "heart," does not occur at lines 4, 13, and 27. The fifth stanza is quite different from that found in the finished poem. A typescript was made from this manuscript, and though this was corrected the poem remained pretty much as in the manuscript until September 1938 when Yeats went to work on it again and created the poem we know. It was among the last to be finished of his

major poems and shows Yeats at work during his last year. The drafts
show that Yeats's discipline, his ability to keep at a poem until it came
right never deserted him. Since this whole study of Yeats at work on
poems is a record of his craftsmanship, a demonstration that he did
not write his poems in a trance though some of them began in dream
visions, an analysis of the composition of "The Circus Animals' Desertion" brings it to an appropriate close.

Below is a list of the drafts of "The Circus Animals' Desertion,"
arranged in what I believe to be the order they were written.

MS. 1*a*.   An early draft of stanza 1 and part of stanza 2.

MS. 1*b*.   Another draft of stanza 1.

MS. 1*c*.   Another draft of stanza 2.

MS. 2.   A manuscript of the whole poem, dated "London
November 1937."

MS. 3.   Another draft of stanza 5, later than MS. 2 but earlier
than TS. 1.

TS. 1.   A transcription of MSS. 2 and 3, with corrections in
WBY's hand.

TS. 2.   A copy of the corrected TS. 1, with further manuscript
corrections. Either WBY or George Yeats has written
on it, "corrected Sept. 15."

TS. 3.   A transcript of TS. 2 as corrected, with new and very
important manuscript changes.

TS. 4.   Another copy with further manuscript corrections, and
a draft of a new fifth stanza in Yeats's hand. WBY has
dated it "corrected Sept 23," and opposite the new
draft has written "insert slip X."

MS. 4.   Has the heading "Slip X." Two further drafts of
stanza 5.

All of these drafts are printed below, and I follow each of them with
my comments.

[MS. 1*a*]

X  For some
   I have sought a theme and sought for it in vain
   And sought for it daily for some five weeks ~~now~~    or so
X  I that/ perhaps
   I am too old — old men alter
X  Something resembling happiness they know

&times; If not happiness itself a show
&times; Of happiness because do not show
   As much of happiness as a man can know
&times; Their minds are full and they no longer strain
&times; Like drowning men and [two words undeciphered] strain
&times; Their minds are too full now for pain and strain
&times; They have no [two words undeciphered] but the care to sow
   For their full minds ~~have~~   may put off pain and strain
   And all poetic themes are plants that grow
   Out of the necessity of a mind
   That were they lacking were but burning sand

[From the verso of this sheet the beginnings of stanza 2.]

   A poem that no matter where it ~~goes~~   seems
   Is ~~but an allegory~~   allegorical like those ancient shows
   Of wretched life, but I set Usheen ride
&times; And I starved for the bosom of his bride
16 ~~And~~   I starved for the bosom of his faery bride.

## [MS. 1*b*]

[From the back of one of the pages of the MS. of "The Municipal Gallery Revisited."]

   I have sought a theme and sought for it in vain
   I have [sought] it daily for five weeks or so
   Perhaps I shall not find it an old man
   Perhaps I am [at] last too old a man
   ~~And~~   I must be ~~content~~   satisfied with fact although
   Last winter dream or theme before me ran
   ~~My~~   As traveling circus all ~~the~~   my beasts on show
&times; Giraffe and men on stilts or in a chariot
&times; Woman and lion and the Lord knows what
   Giraffe, men on stilts, a high chariot
   Giraffe, men upon stilts, or a high chariot
   Lion and woman and Lord knows what

## [MS. 1*c*]

[Another page of jottings for the second stanza.]

   Through those three isles that are in all men's dreams

Through those three ~~islands~~ isles, or ~~allegoric dreams~~  ~~three~~
    ~~perfect dreams~~  or allegoric dreams
X  A journey dance insatiable [?] blows
X  Peace ending wretchedly
Of insatiable [?] joy, insatiable [?] blows
Insatiable [?] peace, ~~three allegoric themes~~  one of those
    themes
The middle ages put into their shows
Or so I think that set on the ride

[All the above cancelled.]

    Yet images were more than life it seems
10  First that sea rider Usheen led by the nose
11  Through three ~~allegorical~~  enchanted islands, allegorical
      ~~dreams~~
Of the emptiness of joy, battle and repose
X  One of those
A summing up of life — one of those themes
The middle ages put in songs and shows
Or so I thought [that] set him on to ride
Starved for the bosom of his faery bride.

Manuscript 1 is, I believe, a very early draft, indeed it may be
Yeats's first draft. It resembles other first drafts in its not quite certain
exploration of materials and structure, in consisting mostly of cancelled lines, and in being extremely difficult to decipher. Already the
stanza pattern of the poem has been determined (ottava rima) and
governs what Yeats writes. He has set the a and b rhyme sounds of
the finished poem (vain, strain; so, know, show), though only "vain,"
"so," and "show" persisted. Yeats later abandoned the c rhyme used
here (mind, sand). Of the matters explored in the finished first stanza
we find only the search for a new theme and Yeats's fear that he is too
old to find one. The circus animals are notably absent. In their place
we find a statement that poetic themes grow out of the necessity of a
mind, which without such growth would be a veritable desert. In the
draft on ms. 1b Yeats makes definite progress. The circus animals
arrive: Yeats has assembled his materials, and he fills out, though in
places rather hurriedly, his intended form. Seven line ends are in place
(vain, so, man, although, show, chariot, what), and although no lines
are quite finished 1, 2, 3, 7, and 8 are nearly so. Two details in this

draft interest me particularly. The first is Yeats's statement that he must be satisfied to have "fact" replace his amazing emblems; it was not until very late in composing the poem that Yeats came to say he must be satisfied with feeling (heart) rather than with the emblems into which he had earlier translated this feeling. The second is the phrase "men upon stilts," both because of the sea-change it undergoes in the later drafts, and because of its anticipation of that rollicking poem, "High Talk."

On the verso of MS. 1a Yeats began work on his second stanza, here telescoped, so to speak, the form not completely filled out. Yeats has decided that the subject of the stanza will be *The Wanderings of Oisin* and his own human situation, that is his longing for love, at the time he wrote it. Yeats has set his rhyme sounds, and the ends of lines 13–16 are in place. Line 16 is done, though Yeats will try other forms of it before finally establishing this form. In MS. 1c Yeats wrote a partial and then a full draft of stanza 2. Yeats now began his stanza by briefly summarizing the action of *Oisin*, and by comparing his allegory with allegories "The middle ages put into their shows." In the full draft Yeats completed his stanza form, set six of his line ends, and completed lines 10 and 11. His preliminary work on this stanza was done.

Manuscript 2, the first surviving draft of the whole poem, has first and second stanzas derived from the drafts just studied. No preliminary drafts of stanzas 3, 4, and 5 seem to have survived, but stanzas 3 and 4 are here more nearly finished than stanzas 1 and 2. It therefore seems certain that earlier drafts of these stanzas, and probably of stanza 5, were made. Though stanza 5 is in this draft more worked over than the others, it contains nothing that Yeats will keep. Yeats tried another draft of this stanza, MS. 3, before having the poem typed.

[MS. 2]

TRAGIC TOYS
THE CIRCUS ANIMALS' DESERTION

I

1 I sought a theme and sought for it in vain
  I have sought it daily for six weeks or so
3 Maybe at last being but an aged   a broken man
  I must be satisfied with life although contented with this heart

[WBY has struck "satisfied with life" then marked it stet.]

5 Winter and summer till ~~this decline~~   old age began
6 My circus animals were all on show,
7 Those stilted boys, that burnished chariot,
8 Lion and woman and the Lord knows what.

II

X Those images ~~were more grand than~~   outglittered life it seems
X For all things counted more than life
X ~~And every toy was~~   Those tragic toys were more than life it
        seems
9 What can I but enumerate old themes
10 First that sea rider Usheen led by the nose
11 Through three enchanted islands, allegorical dreams
    Vain exaltation, battle and repose
    A summing up of life ~~one of those themes~~   or so it seems
14 That might adorn old songs or courtly shows
15 ~~Or so I thought~~   But what cared I that set him ~~up~~   on to ride
16 I starved for the bosom of his fairy bride

III

17 And then a counter truth filled out its play
18 *The Countess Cathleen* was the name I gave it
19 She pity crazed had given her soul away
20 But masterful heaven intervened to save it
21 I thought my dear must her own soul destroy
22 So did fanaticism and hate enslave it
23 And this brought forth a dream and soon enough
    The dream itself had all my thought and love

IV

    And then while Fool and Blindman stole the bread
26 Cuchulain fought the invulnerable sea
    Great mysteries there and yet when all is said
28 It was the dream itself enchanted me:
29 Character isolated by a deed
30 To engross the present and dominate memory.
    The players and the painted stage took all my love
32 And not those things that they were emblems of.

V

&times; Why brood upon old triumphs? Prepare to die
&times; For all those burnished chariots are in flight.
&times; O hours of triumph come and make me gay;
&times; Even at the approach of/ For even on/ For on the edge of
            the   unimagined night
&times; Man has the refuge of his gaiety;
    But lonely to the lone; the   tents blown away
    Women and stilts and chariots all in flight
    Man makes a refuge of his gaiety
    Mocks the approach   Even at the approach of unimagined
            night
    O hour of triumph come and make me gay
    A dab of black enhances every white
    Tension is but the vigour of the mind,
    Cannon the god and father of mankind.
                    London
                November 1937

[MS. 3]

[On a separate sheet WBY wrote another draft of the final stanza which is later than the complete MS. but earlier than TS. 1.]

    Why brood upon old triumphs, prepare to die
&times; Renounce immortality learn to die
    The burnished chariot is wheeled away   from sight
    O hour of triumph come and make me gay
&times; For though the black velvet of unimagined night
&times; Comes I have still my gaiety
    Even at the approach of unimagined night
    Man has the refuge [of his] gaiety
    A dab of black enhances every white
    Tension is but the vigour of the mind
    Cannon the God and father of mankind

Yeats made several interesting changes in this draft of stanza 1 and nearly completed his first eight lines. In line 2 "five weeks" becomes "six weeks," perhaps an indication that draft 1b had been written some days before. Line 3 was greatly improved:

MS. 1b  Perhaps I am [at] last too old a man
MS. 2    Maybe at last being but a broken man.

In line 4, when Yeats wrote and cancelled "contented with this heart," he began to explore the central theme of the finished poem, but for some reason backed away from it. "Satisfied with life," which Yeats allowed to stand, is an advance over "satisfied with fact." Line 5 in MS. 1b read

> Last winter dream or theme before me ran

when Yeats finished line 5 here he has generalized his statement, removed the accidence of the moment from it

> Winter and summer till old age began.

The diction of line 6 has improved amazingly:

MS. 1b  As travelling circus all my beasts on show
MS. 2    My circus animals were all on show.

Knowing that the "stilted boys" of line 7 derived from "men upon stilts" adds a new dimension to the meaning of Yeats's epithet. Oisin and Forgael walk upon stilts, so to speak, but they are also stilted in the more usual, metaphoric sense. Lines 1, 3, 5–8 are done, line 2 nearly done, all the line ends are established.

In stanza 2 Yeats also made great progress. In line 9, "more than life" (1c) becomes "more grand than life," then "outglittered life," "counted more than life," "Those tragic toys were more than life." It was no doubt after he had written the phrase "tragic toys" that Yeats tried at the head of this draft the title "Tragic Toys." Yeats finally dropped all of these descriptions of his emblems in order to express again his lack of a new theme. The line, "What can I but enumerate old themes," is a happy introduction to section 2 of the poem. At line 14 the reference to the Middle Ages in the earlier drafts is absorbed in the epithet "old." All the line ends are set; three additional lines are finished (9, 14, 15); line 16 has again the form of the 1a draft.

Since no earlier drafts of stanzas 3 and 4 have come to light, no study of Yeats's progress is possible. Stanza 3 is finished save for one word in line 24; stanza 4 nearly as far along. I have marked line 26 finished, for I feel certain "Cuchulain fought the invulnerable sea" is the reading Yeats intended. His manuscript is unusually clear at this point; there can be no doubt that he wrote "invulnerable." [4] It is inconceivable that Yeats would consciously back off from this into "ungovernable," though that does fill out the meter and works after a fashion. His typist made the mistake, and Yeats may never have noticed it, given the eye's uncanny ability to see what it expects rather than what is on the page. Here and elsewhere, as I show, Yeats's text could be considerably improved by a study of his manuscripts.

Neither in MS. 2 nor 3 does Yeats achieve even an adumbration of his splendid final stanza. In MS. 2 he recapitulates details from earlier parts of the poem, then goes on to introduce a recollection of "Lapis Lazuli" in the play on "gay" and "gaiety." One is reminded by this typical event of how "The Fisherman" haunted section 3 of "The Tower" many years before. Yeats's anticipation of his own death is too baldly expressed, and the last two rather cryptic lines add little to what he has said elsewhere about the role of violence in human life. In MS. 3 Yeats slightly rearranged his materials and even his lines (3 to 5, 5 to 3), but makes no significant progress. He still has trouble managing his persona, and he has not got rid of echoes from earlier poems.

Typescript 1 was transcribed from MSS. 2 and 3. Then Yeats corrected it, particularly the pointing, in his own hand. I print below this characteristic TS. as corrected.

[TS. 1]
## THE CIRCUS ANIMALS' DESERTION

1  I sought a theme and sought for it in vain,
2  I ~~have~~ sought it daily for six weeks or so.
3  Maybe at last being but a broken man
    I must be satisfied with life, although
5  Winter and summer till old age began
6  My circus animals were all on show,
7  Those stilted boys, that burnished chariot,
8  Lion and woman and the Lord knows what.

9  What can I but enumerate old themes,
10  First that sea-rider Oisin led by the nose
11  Through three enchanted islands, allegorical dreams,
12  Vain ~~exaltation~~ gaiety, vain battle, ~~and~~ vain repose,
    A summing up of life, or so it seems,

14  That might adorn old songs or courtly shows;
15  But what cared I that set him on to ride;
16  I, starved for the bosom of his faery bride.

17  And then a counter truth filled out its play,
18  "The Countess Cathleen" was the name I gave it,
19  She, pity-crazed, had given her soul away
     But masterful heaven intervened to save it.
21  I thought my dear must her own soul destroy
22  So did fanaticism and hate enslave it
23  And this brought forth a dream and soon enough
     The dream itself had all my thought and love.

     And then when Fool and Blind Man stole the bread
26  Cuchulain fought the [ungovernable] sea;
     Great mysteries there, and yet when all is said
28  It was the dream itself enchanted me:
29  Character isolated by a deed
30  To engross the present and dominate memory.
     The players and the painted stage took all my love
32  And not those things that they were emblems of.

×  Why brood upon old triumphs, prepare to die
×  For all those burnished chariots are in flight,
×  What if burnished chariots are put to flight,
×  O hour of triumph come and make me gay.
    O hour of triumph come and make me gay.
    If burnished chariots are put to flight
    Why brood upon old triumph; prepare to die
    Even at the approach of un-imagined night
    Man has the refuge of his gaiety,
    A dab of black enhances every white,
    Tension is but the vigour of the mind,
    Cannon the god and father of mankind.

Yeats finished lines 2 and 12 by correcting TS. 1; the change in
line 12 from "exaltation" to "gaiety" is certainly a preparation for
stanza 5 of this version. The slight rearrangement of the first three
lines of stanza 5 was written out by Yeats and cued into its proper
place. Typescript 2 is a copy of TS. 1 as corrected, except that again
Yeats has written out the revised beginning of stanza 5 and cued it

into place, evidence that those lines were changed after TS. 2 was typed. There is one other manuscript correction: in line 25 "And then when" becomes "And when." With the cancellation of "then" line 25 is finished. More important than these minor changes is the annotation "corrected Sept. 15," probably by George Yeats. (I don't remember Yeats ever putting a period after the abbreviation of a month.) This must mean that TS. 2 represents the state "The Circus Animals' Desertion" had reached in September 1938, ten months after MS. 2 was written.

In TSS. 3 and 4 and in MS. 4 Yeats finished his poem. In TS. 3 Yeats introduces the modal or thematic word of his finished poem when he makes the following changes in his own hand:

4 "satisfied with life" becomes "satisfied with my heart"
13 "A summing up of life" becomes "Themes of the embittered heart" (Yeats first tried another phrase, which I cannot decipher.)
27 "Great mysteries there" becomes "Heart mysteries there"

Yeats then went on to cancel stanza 5, an event for which these changes prepare. He wrote one line of a possible substitute stanza:

Animals and chariots ~~are~~   be still poetic themes.

He also inserted Roman numerals I and II before stanzas 1 and 2 where they are still to be found. Lines 4, 13, and 27 are now finished.

Yeats wrote all the changes noted above into another copy of the poem, which I call TS. 4. At the head of the sheet he experimented further with his title. He cancelled "The Circus Animals' Desertion"; wrote and cancelled "Despair"; wrote "On the Lack of a Theme" and let that stand. He finished line 31 by cancelling "the" before "players" and "painted." He again cancelled stanza 5, wrote a new version of it into the margins of the sheet, and dated it "corrected Sept 23." Here is the new version of stanza 5:

X  The faery woman, Cathleen, Fool and Blind Man
X  Their cousins and their brothers because complete
33 ~~These processional forms~~   Those masterful images
        because complete
34 Grew in pure ~~mind but out of what began?~~   intellect but
        how began
   ~~Out of~~   From the inanimate sweepings of the street,

Bits of old newspaper, that broken can?
X  Or from old rag and bone, that raving slut
   From rag and bone, that raving slut
   Called Heart and Company. My ladder's gone
   And I lie down where all the ladders start
40 In the foul rag and bone shop of the heart.

I think Yeats had invented his splendid final line before he began this draft; the handling of detail in the middle of the stanza seems to point toward it unmistakably. He began by direct allusions to stanzas 2, 3, and 4, then decided to remind his readers of them by two phrases which begin with the demonstrative "those": "Those processional forms/ Those masterful images." No English poet after Spenser has used the allegorical procession so frequently as Yeats; such processions flourish in his poetry from beginning to end. The phrase does evoke *Oisin*, so full of processions, more clearly than *Cathleen* or *On Baile's Strand*, and this may account for the changed reading. Yeats hesitates between "mind" and "intellect" to state the contrast between art and its emotional source, then goes on to explore detail that may be used to describe the rag and bone shop, a process he continues through two later drafts. Yeats in this first draft involves the heart in the rag and bone shop less successfully than later, but his "that raving slut/ Called Heart and Company" does explain what I should have guessed but never had, that the heart keeps the till in the heart's rag-and-bone shop. The ladder that follows, apparently struck off at white heat, is one of Yeats's more complex images. Surely the ladder stands for the pure mind or intellect, the fusing-all-to-one imagination, the faculty which invents the art work. Yeats's splendid final couplet reminds him and us that this art, though a product of pure mind, began of necessity in the accidence of feeling.

Typescript 4 had become so written over that Yeats put in the margin "insert from slip X." I next print Slip X, containing the two final drafts of stanza 5.

[MS. 4]

SLIP X

III

33 Those masterful images because complete
34X Grew in pure mind, but out of what began?

Grew in pure intellect, but ~~where~~ from what began?
~~In this and that~~ ~~Old orange peel, dirt~~ Dirt, orange peel, the
        sweepings of the street
~~Bits of old~~ Old bits [of] newspaper, a broken can,
37 Old iron, old bones, old rags, that raving slut
38 Who keeps the till. Now that my ladder's gone
39 I must lie down where all the ladders start
40 In the foul rag and bone shop of the heart

[WBY cancels the above entire.]

### III

33 Those masterful images because complete
34 Grew in pure mind but out of what began?
35 ~~Dirt, orange peel~~ A mound of refuse or the sweepings of ~~the~~
        a street,
36 Old ~~whiskey bottles~~ kettles, old bottles and a broken can
37 Old iron, old bones, old rags, ~~that~~ the raving slut
38 Who keeps the till. Now that my ladder's gone
39 I must lie down where all the ladders start
40 In the foul rag and bone shop of the heart.

In these final drafts Yeats's progress seems inevitable. He hesitated still between "pure mind" and "pure intellect," finally deciding on "pure mind." He decided also that a general statement followed by detail would put the rag-and-bone shop before us most vividly, and finished line 35 when he wrote "A mound of refuse or the sweepings of a street," then went on to selected detail. He prepares us for the final line by "old bones, old rags," which will be reversed in "rag and bone shop," a device Yeats uses very frequently, and his poem is done except for one word. In line 24 "The dream" became "This dream" sometime before the poem was printed. The new stanza is free of unwanted echoes of his recent work, and Yeats now manages his I-persona in such a way that our thought is transferred from the man Yeats to a phantasmagoric Yeats.

We began to watch Yeats at work upon his poems in 1893; we end in the fall of 1938. In 1893 Yeats's apprenticeship was nearly over; he meticulously completed it shortly after when he reworked his early verse for *Poems*, 1895. Yeats's poetic powers were still as brilliant as ever in September 1938 when he completed "The Circus Animals'

Desertion," though the circle of his activities had necessarily grown narrower.

Yeats was already fully equipped for his sendentary trade when he wrote *The Wind Among the Reeds,* and he never allowed his equipment to rust unused. Early and late he worked at his art strenuously. It is this continued faith in works that in part distinguishes him from lesser poets, that and an unusual ability to stay at a poem until it came right. Yeats himself put it nicely when he quoted from Balzac's *Les Comédiens sans le Savoir* in a little essay which he omitted from *Discoveries:*

Here in Paris, only too often will some artist, seeking Fame that he may have Fortune, seek out some royal road and think to enlarge his stature by identifying himself with some cause, or advocating some system. . . . But while opinion cannot give talent, this mentality spoils it. An artist's opinion ought to be a faith in works.

Such a faith in works Yeats never lost; he made an intense effort, an almost unnatural effort, always to write well.

NOTES

## Notes to Introduction

1    See Jon Stallworthy, *Between the Lines* (Oxford, 1963), pp. 177–200. My "Yeats's Byzantium Poems" was first published in PMLA, March 1960, pp. 110–25, and in a revised form has been twice reprinted. For the details of these reprintings see note 2.

2    Twice in the revised version of my "Yeats's Byzantium Poems," and in Jon Stallworthy's *Between the Lines*, pp. 91–92. Mr. Stallworthy is right (*Between the Lines*, pp. 89–91) when he concludes that I did not know of the existence of these MSS. when I wrote "Yeats's Byzantium Poems"; I first saw them in Dublin in the summer of 1960. The revised version of "Yeats's Byzantium Poems" first appeared in *Yeats: a Collection of Critical Essays*, ed. John Unterecker (Englewood Cliffs, N. J.: Prentice-Hall, 1963) and was reprinted in *Aspects of Poetry*, ed. Mark Linenthal (Boston and Toronto: Little, Brown, 1963), pp. 64–103.

3    Thomas Parkinson studies this ms. on pp. 96–97 of *The Later Poetry*, but does not reproduce it. His observation "The initial notes for the poem . . . are also the notes for stanza 5" led me to develop the argument presented below that the composition of "Among School Children" began in the middle of the finished poem.

4    Mr. Parkinson reproduces part of this ms. in a somewhat different arrangement on pp. 97–98 of *The Later Poetry*.

5    I have stated elsewhere (*Sewanee Review*, Autumn, 1958, pp. 673–74) my conviction that the long line of editors and copy readers who added punctuation to Yeats's own versions of his poems have done us no favor. I now state my conviction again because Jon Stallworthy has recently supported the other view: that Yeats's punctuation needed correction and improvement (*Between the Lines*, pp. 12–13), quoting a letter by Yeats to this effect. I cite as further evidence for my case Yeats's punctuation of "News." With punctuation as with syntax (see *Letters on Poetry*, pp. 192–93) and even meter Yeats was perhaps too diffident about the authority of his own views.

## Notes to Chapter 1

1    Yeats writes in Section XIX and XX of the "First Draft" of his *Autobiographies* that "Into the Twilight" grew out of an estrangement from Maud Gonne, caused in part by a scandalous story about them which was making the rounds in Dublin. Yeats comments: "I went to Sligo seeking to call to myself my courage once again with the lines 'Into the Twilight': Did not the dew shine through love decayed 'Burning in fires of a slanderous tongue'?"

2  Yeats's discussion of "personal utterance" in section xxx of "Reveries over Childhood and Youth" was probably written in 1914.

### Notes to Chapter 2

1  Marion Witt's "The Making of an Elegy," *Modern Philology*, November 1950, indicates that there are MSS. of this poem in the New York Public Library. See p. 117 of her essay.

### Notes to Chapter 4

1  The Slieve Aughty or Echtge Mountains lie directly east of Thoor Ballylee in Co. Galway.
2  I use the word "rhyme" here and elsewhere to stand for assonance or consonance as well as rhyme.
3  The word "Irishry" is an example of how the alchemy of poetry can transmute base metal into gold. Yeats found the word in Toynbee (*The Study of History* — Oxford, 1934 — II, 425). He quotes a passage where Toynbee uses the word in the "Introduction" written for the proposed Dublin Edition and recently printed in *Essays and Introductions*: "He then insists that if 'Jewish Zionism and Irish Nationalism succeed in achieving their aims, then Jewry and Irishry will each fit into its own tiny niche.'" Later in his "Introduction" Yeats himself uses the word "Irishry" several times, always in quotation marks: "[Irish literature] may do something to keep 'the Irishry' living." "It may be indeed that certain characteristics of 'the Irishry' must grow in importance." "I am joined to 'the Irishry.'"

### Notes to Chapter 5

1  Jon Stallworthy prints a transcription of part of the first draft of "Ribh considers Christian Love insufficient" on pp. 10–11 of *Between the Lines*.
2  The notebook may be seen in its original state in a microfilm copy at the Houghton Library, but the contents have since been removed and placed with other MSS. of the works represented.
3  The first named of the three shows this interesting evolution: "craftsman" (item 6), "artist," "workman." Yeats is here moving toward the more inclusive word and at the same time echoing "work" in line 17 of this draft.
4  Yeats's intention here is made more certain still when we observe that in revising "Cuchulain's Fight with the Sea" for *Early Poems and Stories* (1925) Yeats closed the poem with the line "And fought with the invulnerable tide." That "invulnerable" was still echoing in Yeats's mind in this context is proved by these lines from *The Death of Cuchulain* (1939), shortly to be written:

> *Cuchulain.* . . . Then I went mad, I fought against the sea.
> *Aoife.* I seemed invulnerable.